DR. LENDON SMITH'S LOW-STRESS DIET

BOOKS BY LENDON SMITH, M.D.

The Children's Doctor
The Encyclopedia of Baby and Child Care
New Wives' Tales
Improving Your Child's Behavior Chemistry
Feed Your Kids Right
Foods for Healthy Kids
Feed Yourself Right
Dr. Lendon Smith's Low-Stress Diet

DR. LENDON SMITH'S LOW-STRESS DIET

Lendon Smith, M.D.

McGRAW-HILL BOOK COMPANY
New York   St. Louis   Toronto
Mexico   Hamburg   London

This book is not intended to replace the services of a physician. Any application of the recommendations set forth in the following pages is at the reader's discretion and sole risk.

1 2 3 4 5 6 7 8 9 D O C D O C 8 7 6 5 4

ISBN 0-07-058500-8

LIBRARY OF CONGRESS CATALOGING IN PUBLICATION DATA

Smith, Lendon H., 1921-
Dr. Lendon Smith's Low-stress diet.
1. Reducing diets.   2. Reducing—Psychological aspects.   3. Stress (Psychology)—Prevention.   I. Title.   II. Title: Doctor Lendon Smith's Low-stress diet.   III. Title: Low-stress diet.
RM222.2.S6225   1984   613.2′5   84-11223
ISBN 0-07-058500-8

Book design by Roberta Rezk

To my wife, Julie, who slips me a few extra calories now and then just to see if I'll notice. She does it with love, so it's okay.

Acknowledgments

Throughout the book I have used the advice and counsel of some dear, bright friends. They helped share the stress of making this book worthwhile.

Larry Grant of Trail, Oregon, guided me in giving the book the right direction and a logical structure. He pointed out non sequiturs and inconsistencies. I know readers will benefit from his work in clarifying the message of this book.

Anne Condas, a Castro Valley teacher who has made a lifelong study of nutrition, provided me with solid material to help make the book practical and persuasive.

Wayne Anderson, N.D., my naturopathic friend, gave me valuable insights into the workings of the liver, the brain, and the gut. He showed me how they are all connected.

Anastasia Chehak, R.D., of Oklahoma City, Oklahoma, really knows nutrition. She keeps abreast of the latest information in her practice and shares ideas with me. She knows what works.

Bruce MacFarland has had years of experience in the food

and nutrition field. I am grateful for his help in sharpening the concepts and gathering up-to-date information.

Peggy Moss, one of my regulars, has been supportive of my efforts and helpful in getting all this together.

Contents

Introduction: Discovering the Key to Weight Control

They told us in medical school that we were bright, sharp, curious, and energetic people. Our generation of doctors was going to straighten out the world. Then, because each new set of adults would be made normal by our ministrations, these adults would have normal children who would grow up in the path of optimum physical and mental health. There would always be a few accidents and birth anomalies requiring surgery, but everyone would be able to achieve his or her genetic potential free of anxiety, disease, drug dependency, and excess fat. I envisioned a healthy population of trim persons coping success-fully with everyday stresses. With the help of the pharmaceutical houses, we were rapidly approaching the time when every dis-ease would have a specific remedy, whether it was medicine, surgery, or psychiatric counseling: our job was to make the di-agnosis, and look up the treatment in the index. We were taught, therefore, to be superb diagnosticians.

I loved medical school. I got good grades and really believed that I was in the best profession to fulfill my lifelong desire of helping people and having as many people as possible like me. I even tried being a psychiatrist for a while as a means to reaching that goal. I didn't particularly care for that specialty, however, because it seemed that none of my patients were getting well very fast. I needed the positive feedback of quick successes that many doctors strive for.

Maybe obstetrics would be a more rewarding line; it is certainly where life begins—at least for the offspring. Maybe I could help these people more effectively because I would have them at the beginning. My first patient in my obstetrics rotation as an intern developed a postpartum psychosis. Cross obstetrics off the list.

Pediatrics fit the bill very well. The history of the illnesses was short, and the examinations did not take long. The children often got well themselves, sometimes despite their doctors' treatments. So I opted for that specialty. To qualify for board certification, only two years of residency training were required after the rotating internship.

The practice of pediatrics was somewhat stressful, but rewarding. The parents were bringing children in to see me, but the little cuties did not have the diseases I was trained to treat. The patients would sit staring at me, defying me to make a scientific diagnosis when there was nothing that I could find during the examination or any clue in the laboratory reports. But the mother always knew there was a problem. "He doesn't feel good." "She won't eat." "He refuses the milk." "He is full of gas." "She wakes up at night." "Is he hyperactive?" It was nice to have a patient come in with a red, bulging eardrum and a fever. *There* was something you could get your hands on.

During the time that my practice was growing, my wife and I were rearing five children, so we had a chance to put theory into practice. We could not believe that our child-rearing practices—adequate, at least—were responsible for their occasional noncompliant behavior and habits. One sucked a nipple forever, one flopped around, one had to rub the satin edge of the blanket on his nose. One was a bed-wetter, and one had to rock the bed. We had heard that such traits in children meant they were insecure. But, heavens! We could not take the blame for all this psychiatric deviancy. If they walked on their heels and upset us, did they do it because they knew they upset us? Or did they have a need to walk on their heels? Maybe they did not feel good.

We tried to find organic or physiological reasons for their vexing mischief. Pinworms was a good one and helped to explain squirmy wakefulness. Anemia is often the cause of touchiness; it is common in milk-drinking, fast-growing children. Food allergies were behind a host of irritations, including bed-wetting, ear infections, odd rashes, gas, and headaches. These ideas, learned in the domestic laboratory, I applied to my patients. The mothers were delighted, because many nasty, maddening problems were solved and no one had to feel guilty.

To locate sources of allergies, I soon learned to listen to the mothers (and sometimes to the fathers) for the real diagnosis. If I let them talk long enough, they told me the reason for the sickness or the behavior or the symptoms. I was doing independent detective work, which was fun, but it didn't seem to have much to do with what I had learned in medical school. For example, if a child seemed fussy and there was no fever, I could make a diagnosis more readily by asking the mother what the child had eaten in the last few days. I often found confirmatory evidence when I looked at the skin around the child's anus. If there was a red circle of inflamed skin there, then I knew it was a food sensitivity. And the same food that was causing the rash was probably causing the fussiness, the headache, the lethargy, and whatever.

So, although medical school had taught me a number of things, it hadn't covered the little, nit-picking, daily irritations that people have to live with. I also noticed that whenever lay people form a mutual support organization to study and learn about a disease, they are obviously doing so because the medical profession as a group has failed to solve that problem, or perhaps even to address itself to the condition. Alcoholics Anonymous was put together because the medical profession had little but scorn for those weak sufferers. The Arthritis Foundation, the Epilepsy League, and the Muscular Dystrophy Association are but a few of the groups formed to help the victims of chronic debilitating conditions. (I have not heard of a club for appendicitis sufferers or ex-pneumonia patients. Either they make it or they don't.)

The plethora of groups concerned with the problem of overweight attests to the lack of help for the obese that has come from orthodox medicine. In nutrition and health classes in school you were told to drink a quart of milk a day and eat something from the other three groups and all would be well. That was fine, but it didn't work. It took me a few years in practice to understand that we are all very different from one another and yet all very much the same. I was disbelieving when one mother would tell me that her fat child ate nothing, and the very next patient would be a thin, restless type who ate six huge meals a day. They were lying, I decided, or the school was fibbing. If not, it had to mean that people are different. I was getting my first clues as to why some children—and adults—become obese on the same food that allow others to stay thin.

It was after I changed the diets of many hyperactive children that I discovered at least one difference in people: the way their intestines work. I had the children stop the sugary junk and the white flour nothings, discontinue the dairy products for at least a month, take a few B-complex vitamins and some calcium and magnesium, and nibble on fruit, vegetables, whole grains, nuts, and seeds. Almost all the mothers would report after a month, "He feels better, he's stopped punching his sister, his allergy is gone, he smells better, he has less gas, and he needs less food to keep going."

Aha, I thought, that's an absorption problem. Those little

lining cells are not getting the nourishment they need, so they don't work the way they should. I had to give vitamin shots to get the enzymes working. I didn't know it then, but I was balancing the bodies of these children. Once I got everything working well with injections, the kids could do it for themselves orally.

I began to realize that when someone is sick, it is the body telling its owner that there is a tilt, a screw-up in the homeostatic mechanisms; the mechanisms are not working well enough to counteract the stress forces of the environment or the diet.

As a physician, I wanted to help people with their symptoms. A shot of ampicillin brought relief from an earache in about eight hours; the fever of pneumonia dropped from 104° to 100° in about ten to twelve hours after the penicillin injection. Usually it was easy to motivate parents and some of their children to take these miracle-working drugs. People want quick relief and the drugs are truly miracle workers. All the new antibiotics, antihistamines, antihypertensives, anticonvulsants, anti-inflammatories, and antidepressives really work. But because they are so valuable and so exciting, they have tended to distract us from the burning question: *Why does the patient need these things in the first place?* What is making him or her sick, tired, obese?

Obesity is but a symptom. It means that something is wrong. Treating the obesity with drugs or lectures is a mistake. Instead, we have to find the force that is changing the physiology enough to lead to the weight gain.

The work of Dr. Hans Selye has shown us where to look for the answer. Selye was the first to codify the physiological mechanisms of the body in response to perceived stress. Stress is everywhere: home, school, "friends," job, weather, taxes, traffic, going to the bathroom ("Is it going to work one more time?"), getting out of bed, and trying to be a nice person under pressure. Our sense of right and wrong and our need to cope with our own internalized standards are stressors. But stress must be *perceived as stress* by the nervous system before the nerves are activated and the chemicals secreted that produce the effects on the end organs that tell us something has happened. (Rapid heart rate, tight muscles, and that "all gone" feeling are typical effects.) Suicide is not an appropriate or natural way out. More usually a person will go to sleep, throw a tantrum, get an ulcer, or overeat as a response to stress. Some reactions are more damaging to health than others.

I began to work on the idea that stress can cause susceptible people to gain weight. I devised a questionnaire and tried it out on cab drivers. I figured that I would get the quickest and best answers from them. They must have stress, I reasoned, and the older ones frequently were overweight. (If a person looks overweight, he or she *is* overweight.)

My survey of fifty to sixty cab drivers around the country has indicated that only about half had been restless and hyperactive as children in school. (I had expected a higher rate, since driving a vehicle seems like an ideal lifetime job for hyper kids who like to keep moving.) About 80 percent of the drivers love their job despite drunks throwing up on the back seat, robberies, call girls wanting to do an exchange, people who insult and demean them, and no-shows. (Wouldn't the fear of getting mugged make them anxious most of the time?)

The ones who had the fewest symptoms (who noticed stress the least, who had no ulcers, hypertension, muscle aches, tooth decay, allergies, insomnia, or anxiety, and who were thin) were the ones who carried raw vegetables and raw fruit, ate whole-grain bread in their sandwiches, ate fowl, fish, nuts, and seeds. In general, the healthy, thin ones took daily 1000 mg of vitamin C, a B-complex and an all-purpose vitamin and mineral supplement along with calcium and magnesium. They also exercised. Most had stopped smoking. They did not go to fast-food diners and they drank little coffee. The findings reinforced my ideas about the way diet can affect our perception of stress and how stress can lead to overweight in susceptible people.

I would guess that you, reader, are overweight, or you wouldn't be reading this book. You have tried in the past to control your poundage, and maybe you succeeded for awhile, but now your hungry cells have gotten the upper hand. You feel frustrated that you can't seem to change, and you are probably worried too, because you have read that obesity is unhealthy—more fat people than thin people get heart disease, strokes, high blood pressure, hardening of the arteries, cancer, and many other illnesses. So you buy another diet book and try another reducing scheme.

There must be twenty subgroups of heavy people all searching for their ideal weight-control method. Each method will work on *some* people, but no one diet works on all. *We are all different!*

So here (gulp!) is another diet and weight control book. What this book is all about and the essential feature you are to extract from it is that obesity is nothing other than a symptom of a physiological torque. Your brain and your body are connected. It's a two-way street; not only can mental and emotional stress give rise to physical disease, but mental and emotional disorders can *result* from physical disturbances. The soma reacts to the psyche and vice versa. Somatic and mental symptoms—even "insignificant" ones—are the body's way to alert the owner that a biochemical deviation has occurred.

Now, we know that infants and children (you were one once) have traits, conditions, and diseases that are predictive of adult problems and illnesses. We also know that stresses can allow genetic traits to appear. Genes determine the form of the disease, whether it is obesity, eczema, asthma, colitis, arthritis, or migraine, but the reason the disease appears seems to be the lifestyle and the diet acting negatively upon the body. The disease is telling the owner of the body—you—that a metabolic screw-up has occurred. Treating the symptoms is begging the issue. What you need are diet and exercise to balance the body to the point where the symptoms will disappear—most of the time.

One purpose of this book, then, is to give you some reasonably reliable information about how the body works so that you can choose a logical preventive course of action to balance your body and lose symptoms and unneeded weight. (Some of the news might not be comforting, like: "If you love something, it is probably bad for you, as it may be giving you allergic reactions.")

Most weight-loss programs are concerned with the twin approach of calorie restriction and aerobic exercise. These programs are excellent as far as they go, but the poor results over the long term suggest that they are not sufficient in themselves. The body cannot be balanced properly until the problems of stress and nutritional depletion are addressed. Achieving control over the body can only be done through an approach that takes account of the emotions as well as the ingested calories. This is the aim of the program set forth in this book. It is designed to help dieters realize that they are not stuck forever with those extra pounds, that they can exercise freedom of choice and learn to make sound body management part of their lifestyle. It reassures people that they are entitled to feel stress in common life situations and in their jobs, and it tells how to support the body nutritionally so that it can survive the particular stresses and notice them less.

The prudent owner of an overweight body will make some minor adjustments in diet, exercise, habit patterns, and general outlook. If taken early, these measures are usually sufficient in order to return physiological mechanisms to their normal balanced functioning (homeostasis). Making these changes should be as easy and natural as drinking when thirsty, sleeping when tired, and dropping a hot potato. You are to figure out the reason for the poor weight management. If we know whence we came, what illnesses our ancestors had, what our mother was doing and thinking during her pregnancy with us, what problems we had as children, and what makes us, as adults, grind our teeth or chew our nails, then we should be able to avoid the diet and the stresses that are flipping the switches that allow us to be sick, tired, and fat. Proper nutrition and stress control should help us get out of the genetics/stress trap and into some smaller clothes.

My Dad and I shared similar traits and interests. He drank rum and Coke and ate salted peanuts and died of high blood pressure and a stroke. I want to avoid a similar course, so I eat raw nuts and drink only a little white wine. Blood pressure okay. See?

1

Understanding Obesity

Obesity has been studied by some of the brightest minds in and out of medicine, and everyone seems to have a different idea of what obesity is and how to cure it.

Exercise physiologists tell us that burning up excess calories and fat is the best way to lose weight and that diet plays only a secondary role.

Dieticians tend to believe that if one eats three meals a day containing something from each of the four basic food groups, the body will seek out and settle at the ideal—perhaps normal—weight. Weight loss, they say, is simply a matter of cutting down on the calories.

Geneticists would have us believe that our chromosomes are so persuasive that we will fill out to our potential weight and then remain at that, plus or minus 10 pounds, for our entire adult life. They point to the evidence that when both parents are heavy, 80 percent of their children will have overweight problems, while if both parents are thin, only 7 percent will be so burdened. If one parent is obese, 40 percent of the children will have the tendency for life.

Pathophysiologists, like the late Dr. William Sheldon, are interested in abnormal function as related to structure. Dr. Sheldon felt the genetic trait common to the overweight is a long intestinal tract. In long, thin body types, called ectomorphs, the length of the gut is but a mere 20 feet. Their breakfast might be down at the sigmoid by midafternoon. Not much time to absorb the calories. Heavy folk, however, can have up to 40 feet of intestine, which gives them more time to absorb and a few more acres of absorptive surface to soak and store up every smidgeon of fat and sugar. These endomorphs usually have thick lips and short, tapering fingers. A third body type, the mesomorphs, have 30 feet of bowel and tend to be more muscular, or, at least, neither fat nor thin.

Another theory has it that humans can be divided into carnivores (those who should eat meat predominantly), herbivores (vegetarians), and omnivores (those who eat a little of everything). Most of us are of the latter group and do well on a varied diet following the principles of the four basic food groups. If you have discovered that you do well nibbling, then it suggests that you are a herbivore and your ancestors worked their way through the jungle on bark, berries, nuts, fruits, and leaves. Keep it up; just remember not to nibble on meat, fat, or quick sugary junk.

If you are of the carnivorous type, you may have discovered that you do better eating one meal a day and are nauseated if you have to eat more. But you cannot eat nutrient-poor foods or you will get fat.[1] In general, those who get by on one meal a day tend to gain fat and lose lean muscle tissue, while the

1. David Jones, M.D., and Doris Jones, F.R.A.I., "Obesity; Separating the Herbivores from the Carnivores," *Modern Medicine* (15 May 1976), pp. 84–90.

nibblers are more likely to maintain a more or less ideal weight.

Neurologists and animal research physiologists usually blame obesity on lesions in the lower midbrain (hypothalamus) that cause increased appetite and decreased activity. The heavier one becomes, the more difficult it is to move. And with less exercise, even more weight accumulates along with a bad self-image and the "I don't care!" attitude that many of us have experienced.

Psychiatrists have had a field day with the emotional problems of the obese. But many of them are honest enough to admit that the disturbed psyche may be the *result* of the obese condition just as commonly as it is the cause. Those who feel themselves overweight are naturally prey to discouragement, frustration, and the sense of having lost control. Stress, or the perception of stress, can make the blood sugar fall, and that triggers the desire to eat. Eating makes the heavies feel guilty and reinforces their perception of themselves as weak and out of control. Their depression, in many cases, is the emotional consequence of a physical condition (obesity).

There is even some difference of opinion as to the definition of "obese." Most of us who are used to living inside our own bodies can tell very simply whether we are fat or thin. If we look in the mirror and the image looks fat, we are probably fat. If we look thin, we are thin. (This does not apply to people with anorexia nervosa, who usually have a dysperception that they are fat.)

Years ago, life insurance companies constructed tables indicating ideal weight for height. Their actuarial statistics showed that if people were either too fat or too thin, they died earlier. Each 10 pounds over the ideal was supposed to shorten the life of the burdened by one year. Those whose height and weight came within the guidelines had the best chance of survival.

In 1983, after years of following the heavy ones through life and rechecking the findings, the insurance experts revised the tables upward. Now they believe that a little extra weight is

MEN

Height Feet	Inches	Small Frame	Medium Frame	Large Frame
5	2	128-134	131-141	138-150
5	3	130-136	133-143	140-153
5	4	132-138	135-145	142-156
5	5	134-140	137-148	144-160
5	6	136-142	139-151	146-164
5	7	138-145	142-154	149-168
5	8	140-148	145-157	152-172
5	9	142-151	148-160	155-176
5	10	144-154	151-163	158-180
5	11	146-157	154-166	161-184
6	0	149-160	157-170	164-188
6	1	152-164	160-174	168-192
6	2	155-168	164-178	172-197
6	3	158-172	167-182	176-202
6	4	162-176	171-187	181-207

Weights at Ages 25-59 Based on Lowest Mortality. Weight in Pounds According to Frame (in indoor clothing weighing 5 lbs., shoes with 1" heels).

WOMEN

Height Feet	Inches	Small Frame	Medium Frame	Large Frame
4	10	102-111	109-121	118-131
4	11	103-113	111-123	120-134
5	0	104-115	113-126	122-137
5	1	106-118	115-129	125-140
5	2	108-121	118-132	128-143
5	3	111-124	121-135	131-147
5	4	114-127	124-138	134-151
5	5	117-130	127-141	137-155
5	6	120-133	130-144	140-159
5	7	123-136	133-147	143-163
5	8	126-139	136-150	146-167
5	9	129-142	139-153	149-170
5	10	132-145	142-156	152-173
5	11	135-148	145-159	155-176
6	0	138-151	148-162	158-179

Weights at Ages 25-59 Based on Lowest Mortality. Weight in Pounds According to Frame (in indoor clothing weighing 3 lbs., shoes with 1" heels).

Source of basic data: 1979 Build Study, Society of Actuaries and Association of Life Insurance Medical Directors of America, 1980.
Metropolitan Life Insurance Company Ideal Weight for Height Chart

compatible with a long, happy, and reasonably disease-free life. A *little* extra weight, that is, but not too much.

In most studies of the obese, the criterion for entry into the program is a weight 20 percent greater than the Metropolitan Life Insurance Company figures. If you are a 5-foot-3-inch female with a medium frame, the table says that your ideal weight is between 121 and 135 pounds. Twenty percent of 130 is 26. So if you weigh more than 130 plus 26 (156 pounds), you are eligible to be called obese and are at risk for diabetes, cardiovascular disease, cancer, and osteoarthritis. We have to draw the line somewhere. We have to have rules.

Find yourself on the chart and see how you are doing. Notice that the weights on the tables *include* clothing—if you weigh yourself stripped, you're cheating a little. Are you uncomfortable with your weight, and over the upper limit the table is willing to grant you by 20 percent or more? If so, you should try to lose.

But first you must do a little research into your past and find out how well you score on the key factors that influence weight control. With this knowledge, you can choose the diet that is right for you, the one that will help you lose the symptom of obesity—*forever.*

FACTORS THAT INFLUENCE WEIGHT CONTROL

We are all different, and what works for one person may not work on another. In his book *Biochemical Individuality,* Dr. Roger J. Williams has described how genetics, pregnancy factors, environmental influences, perception of stress, accidents, allergies, and pollutants can all distort one's physiology.[2] We know that a weight control program must be individualized to take these factors into account.

2. Austin: University of Texas Press, 1977.

Genetics

Look at your parents and grandparents (or look at pictures of them). Are most of them heavy? Do they have short, tapering fingers and thick lips? Is there diabetes, hypertension, cancer, allergy, osteoarthritis, and cardiovascular disease in many of them? Now, if your ancestors all exhibit these problems and clues, it does not mean you are stuck with the family curse. However, it does suggest that your struggle with your body will require some supports for your enzyme systems and a long-term commitment to preventive maintenance.

Your family name could be a clue to your biochemical individuality. What tribe, region, or country nourished your ancestors? Someone of Oriental background might do better with quick-fried vegetables and rice. I can live on scones, haggis, and an occasional piece of fish. My Scot ancestors survived on this type of food. (Did they leave the Highlands because of politics, or was it the boring food?) If you are an Eskimo, you should pattern your diet to the general types of food that allowed your ancestors to survive—fish, mainly. The one factor common to both the Eskimo and the Japanese diet is the amount of cold-water fatty fish in the diet. They eat a fairly large amount of herring, cod, haddock and mackerel. The Eskimos who now are eating processed food, white bread, and homogenized milk are sick with ear infections, obesity, and depression. The Masai in Kenya drink milk and blood from their cattle. Why don't they get milk allergies? Is it because the milk is fresh? Nathan Pritikin tells us that the diet of the Masai is rich in fat. They do have cholesterol deposits on their blood vessels, but because they exercise so much, herding their cows and goats, their blood vessels are abnormally large and the few plaques they get do not cause obstructions.

Many Greeks survive into old age. They are physically active and use 3 to 4 ounces of olive oil daily. Unfortunately, no one has found that the high-fat, high-sugar, low-roughage diet of Americans helps promote disease-free longevity.

Gestation

Was your mother under sixteen years old or over thirty-eight when you were born? Such timing is a stress for both mother and infant. (Can you imagine being pregnant at age forty and anticipating the next eighteen years of the PTA?) Did she have you within two years of an earlier sibling's birth or an earlier pregnancy? These stresses exhaust not just the adrenal glands of the mother but the adrenals of the baby as well.

Is there any way you can find out about your mother's diet when she was carrying you? Did she have nausea and vomiting? If she did, it suggests that she was low in B_6 and you consequently could have been deprived of this important nutrient. Sometimes a pregnant woman's nausea is a clue that she is prone to hypoglycemia, which can run rampant through families.

Did she have muscle cramps? (Most women remember how uncomfortable they were during pregnancy if they had muscle cramps or back aches.) If she did, it suggests that you might have been cheated in your supply of calcium and magnesium. You could ask her where she got her calcium. She might reply that she drank a quart of milk every day like her obstetrician told her to do. So why did she get cramps if she swallowed the calcium? Because swallowing is not the same as absorbing. If calcium and magnesium were low in the infant because they didn't go through the placenta, then you, the infant, were put in jeopardy of increased perception of stress, and that could push you into compulsive eating as an adult.

Did she have physical stress, or an illness, accident, or operation during her pregnancy with you? Did she hate the whole idea of the pregnancy with you? Would she tell you now if she did? Was she pregnant by the right man? Negatives like these often lead to stress, which promotes allergies in the baby—and allergies can distort the physiology enough to allow obesity to occur.

It appears that an allergy-prone woman who eats some food frequently and abundantly may induce an enzyme system in the offspring she is carrying. When the baby after delivery eats this same food, he or she may respond rather violently because the immune system was set up to react. If a mother eats a great quantity of sugar, the baby may overreact with insulin when sugar is ingested in infancy. This overresponse of the pancreas might set up the craving and the inability to turn away from the goodies in later life. If the mother drinks much milk on the assumption that it is a good thing to build her baby's bones, she might only be setting up a milk allergy in her child.

Did your mother deliver you prematurely? Premature birth is associated with milk allergy and sensitivities in general. An allergic fetus may become hyperactive while still in the uterus and trigger an early delivery. The child is a target for allergies because of the stress to the mother that led to the premature birth. Then, because of the nature of the post-delivery care, the baby may not be fed at its mother's breast. But in this situation the need for breast-feeding is almost an emergency. Many premature nurseries are recognizing this fact and are setting up human milk banks for the wee ones. The babies grow better on it, they have fewer infections, and they seem to be less allergic. Despite all this, they are prone to asthma, eczema, hay fever, and respiratory infections. The stress of their early delivery allows them to get a stress-related disease, and the stress further depletes the adrenals so that the stress perpetuates the disease which acts as a stress and leads to the continuation of the disease.

Calcium seems to be deficient in those with asthma, hypertension, and eczema. The rapidly growing preemie may not get enough calcium from the milk he drinks; if he is allergic to milk, he may get very little calcium from it. Stress from illness and food allergies causes the blood sugar to drop and encourages hunger. Calcium levels in the blood also fall when the blood sugar drops; this could lower the threshold for sensitivity. The calcium-deficient person often perceives stress more easily.

Many do not realize that the allergies they thought they had outgrown as children are still plaguing them, albeit in a new form. The wheat that caused a flare-up in a child's eczema may now, in this child's adult body, cause gas, weight gain, and an itchy anal area. The milk allergy that allowed ear infections and bronchitis in a toddler might cause bloody noses, muscle cramps, and weight gain in the adult. Anything can do anything. It is usually the most loved food that is responsible.

It is important to dwell on the stresses and problems of the pregnancy because so many allergies are started in those first months. The pregnancy is like the launching pad. If given the right lift during those nine months, the child may soar through life with few problems because he or she has been put together properly.

People in primitive societies seemed to be aware of the deleterious effects of a stressful pregnancy. When a woman became pregnant the tribe would surround her with all sorts of support. She got the best food. She was treated as a queen.

We should do more for pregnant women in our culture. Maybe there should be a phone number women could call where they would hear a supportive message, even if it was only a tape: "We love you. You are doing great. Keep it up."

Birth, Nursing, and the First Year

It would be important to find out from your parents and whoever delivered you about the stresses and strains during the delivery. Some babies become allergic, some hyperactive, some brain-damaged, and some frankly retarded due to a tumultuous delivery. An occasional baby might suffer some bleeding in the part of the lower brain (hypothalamus) that controls food intake; his "appestat" is destroyed. He eats forever; he gets and stays fat.

This initial passage, even when "normal," must be one of the most stressful events we will ever experience. It is hard on mother and baby, but the baby can forgive the world for this trauma if he or she gets comforted and cuddled right away. Recent research indicates that the birth is best followed by skin contact, warmth, and food. The baby should be put naked against the mother's chest and allowed to find a breast. Mother Nature allows two choices, both perfect.

Somehow modern medicine decided to interfere with this beautiful, natural relationship. The cold atmosphere of science took over, and with it came stress, allergies, insecure babies, and confused mothers. Keep the mother and infant separate, science said. Let the nursery clean up the baby, take its temperature, and give it sugar water so it won't get dehydrated. At the same time, the mother is to be sedated or anesthetized so the episiotomy can be sutured. With the drugs in her she may not know or care if she had a baby.

All this is disruptive to the natural biological and hormonal functions that Mother Nature has provided to establish breast-feeding and the mother-child bond. Centuries of experimenting have failed to produce a milk that can compare with human milk for human babies. We were taught in medical school about evaporated milk formulas: add water and syrup and the baby would grow. And they did. I look back now and shudder. It is a dead milk. It is designed for an animal that has a large body and a small brain. If pasteurized milk is offered to a calf as its first milk, it either refuses it or is dead in six weeks of the scours (a malignant form of diarrhea). What are we doing to our babies?

Breast milk is alive. It has all the proper constituents for life, growth, and health. The early colostrum, the mother's first milk, has about the same number of white blood cells as the mother's blood. This "seeds" the baby's immune system.

Breast-fed babies eat frequently, are often up at night, and are usually cute and fat. Doctors used to think that this early obesity would lead to obesity in the adult, but long-term studies have indicated that only about 10 percent of fat, breast-fed babies ended up as fat adults.[3] (Genetic influence?) The problem babies were more likely the bottle-fed ones and those put on solids early.

Bottle-fed babies are doubly at risk. It is not just the stress of the cow's milk, but also the stress—whatever it is—that is preventing the mother from nursing. An unsupportive doctor, an indifferent husband, a regimented hospital that won't let the La Leche League come in to instruct the mothers, a surly nurse— all these are stresses and should be avoided. No wonder there has been such an increase in non–hospital-based birthing hospices. Women feel they have some autonomy in these places.

Accumulated stresses exhaust the baby's adrenals and set up the biochemistry that allows him to be allergic; if it is cow's milk he is getting, it is cow's milk to which he will be allergic. The point is that allergies often lead to hypoglycemia and hypoglycemia can set up the chemistry of unwanted weight gain.

In the 1920s and 1930s general practitioners and the new army of pediatricians were becoming concerned about "milk anemia." Babies on cow's-milk formula did not get enough iron and were quite anemic by one year of age. My Dad, the pediatrician, had mothers scrape cooked beef for the baby at about twelve months of age. Then Gerber, Heinz, and Beechnut joined the hue and cry—"start solids early"—to prevent the anemia. The race was on. Within a decade or two the early feeding of solids got to be a status indicator for young mothers: "I started my baby on rice and applesauce at three weeks." Some at least waited until the cord was tied. Most of those who were fed solids early avoided the anemia, but a new problem cropped up. (There always seems to be a trade-off in medicine.) Feeding them solids

3. Lewis A. Barnes, M.D., et al. (Committee on Nutrition, American Academy of Pediatrics), "Nutritional Aspects of Obesity," *Pediatrics*, June 1982, pp. 880–882.

pushed some of these babies into an allergic status which they were never able to outgrow.

Babies do not have the enzyme systems to break down solid foods into the basic amino acids, simple carbohydrates, and fatty acids. Some of these foods are absorbed only partially digested, and the peptides that are formed act on the body as allergens. The body sets up an allergic reaction which may last a lifetime. Remember: 80 percent of those with food allergies have hypoglycemia, and this can lead to obesity. Are pediatricians responsible for the present heavy generation? Maybe.

If you are heavy now, find out from your mother when she started you on solids. Did you have reactions from soy milk or eggs or wheat or whatever? A rash from cow's milk during babyhood may be a clue that cow's milk is now causing obesity. "Eat it today and wear it tomorrow" applies to rashes as well as avoirdupois.

If you had ear infections, colic, rashes, croup, runny nose, asthma, diarrhea, constipation—almost any persistent symptom—as an infant, you were probably allergic to some food; usually it was cow's milk. You may think you have outgrown it by now, but it may have just moved to another system. My childhood mastoid infection, bed-wetting, and constipation from milk are now bloody noses, gas, and postnasal drip. The colic or asthma you got from wheat as an infant may now have moved to headaches, anxiety, and obesity—especially if you now love bread, pasta, and wheat cereal. It has been discovered that in some people alcoholism is due to an allergy to the botanical source of the alcohol, e.g., wheat, rye, malt, hops, etc.

Childhood

The tendency to heaviness from the age of five years to ten years is a reliable predictor of an adult tendency to obesity.[4]

4. Ibid.

This is due evidently to combined genetic, physiological, and anatomical factors. If you only got chunky at puberty or early adolescence, you should find it easier to manage your body weight at the ideal level once you have arrived at age twenty. But if you remember being a chubby first- or fourth- or fifth-grader, and you are back into the lard again, it doesn't necessarily mean you are a hopeless case. It just suggests that you will have to work a little harder at losing.

If you remember being very thin as a child despite a huge appetite (the hollow-leg syndrome), but you are now gaining on the same intake and you are still exercising, it could mean that your absorptive mechanisms have improved, that your thyroid is slowing down, or that you are now allergic to some food.

Absorption

I am amazed at how much sugar and starch hyperactive kids can scarf down, yet they are almost always thin, really thin. I used to think they stayed thin because they burned up the calories faster than they swallowed them. But after I began treating them with a nutritional approach, I learned that absorption is the key to their problem and to many other problems with diverse symptoms. The mothers almost inevitably reported a simultaneous decrease in food intake and an increase in weight after about a month of no sugar, no white flour, and extra vitamin B complex, C, calcium, and magnesium. The children's perpetual motion did calm down, but not enough to explain the "need" for fewer calories and the moderate weight gain. Most of them showed improvement if I had them stop ingestion of all dairy products for the month.

I assume I was "normalizing" the body chemistry by providing the nutrients that are required by the absorbing cells in the lining of the intestines, thus enabling them to work better and absorb more. One theory of obesity blames it on our modern diet; our foods are so calorie-rich and nutrient-poor that the body keeps on eating to get the vitamins and minerals it needs and inadvertently gets too many calories since it absorbs more of what it doesn't need.

Some doctors put these hyperactive, thin kids on digestive enzymes, with calming effect. The kids seem to be able to absorb the nutrients they need, as the swallowed enzymes break the foods down into the simple sugars, fatty acids, and amino acids. These simple food elements are nonallergenic.

We know one of the keys to maintaining normal weight, staying healthy, having enough energy, getting restful sleep, handling stress, and avoiding mood swings. It is this: Provide the body's enzymes with the proper vitamins and minerals for that particular, unique body, and the body will organize itself into the efficient machine it was meant to be. These enzymes need the vitamins and minerals to operate effectively. But the enzymes cannot pick up the vitamins and minerals out of the foods unless the enzymes are operating effectively. A Catch-22.

Vitamin injections may be necessary to get the system going until it becomes efficient enough to continue without this intervention. Herbal products can be effective here because they are better absorbed and their vitamins, minerals, and organic chemicals work synergistically; that is, they work better in combination than they would as separate ingredients taken alone. Herbalists and naturopaths often use the following to improve liver function: lecithin (one tablespoon of the granules), choline (1000 mg), methionine (1000 mg), vitamin B_6 (50 to 100 mg), vitamin B_{12} (30 mcg), iodine (225 mcg), and magnesium (100 mg). Brewer's yeast seems helpful, as well as the herbs taraxicum, cheledonium majus, Russian black radish, and beet leaf.

Psychogenic Factors

Did your parents and grandparents reward you with candy when they were proud of you? Did you get these same delights when you were hurt, frightened, or depressed? It has been assumed until recently that obesity in adulthood is based on a learned response: eat sugar in response to any emotion.

There is no denying that eating has some degree of emotional content. But as any normal parent has observed, energy lifts and the mood improves in response to almost any food. "Well, you're just hungry," is the usual comment to explain late-afternoon surliness and fighting with siblings. The quicker the energy source, the speedier the return of cheerfulness. The parents are rewarded for feeding the children cookies, and, of course, the children learn something too.

Apparently, however, most parents are not correlating the "return of the monster" with the subsequent fall of the blood sugar about one to three hours after the sugar ingestion. They say, "You're bad," give the child a wallop, and send him off to bed without his supper—probably the only thing that would have returned him to cheerful compliance and humaneness.

What the child may learn from this is that sugar is therapy and his parents are capricious. By the time he is an adult he may have developed a bad self-image, and when any emotion wells up (fear, anxiety, depression, insomnia, worry), he may resort to food.

A biochemical response will reinforce a psychiatric stress. Any stress will make the blood sugar drop, and this drop is the trigger to the brain's appetite center to initiate foraging for food. During the time the blood sugar is falling, the cortex of the brain is not fully operative. Apparently, reduction of energy flow through this part of the brain that has to do with self-control and self-image will allow the lower centers of the brain to have their way. "I don't care" and "I'll start tomorrow" are examples of selfish, animal, spinal-cord thinking. ("I'll just have *one* chocolate out of the box." Sure!)

Here's a good example of the interrelationship of foods and stress from the files of the Page Clinic in Saint Petersburg Beach, Florida.

Jane, an incurable snacker since the death of her husband,

had gained 30 pounds in the last three years. A Heidelberg acid/ alkali test of her digestive juices revealed that she had an over-abundance of stomach acid. She also had genetically overactive adrenal glands. Stress stimulated her stomach to squirt out the acid and the adrenals to pump out their hormones. The pancreas could not secrete enough alkali (bicarbonate) to neutralize the acid when the food moved from the stomach to the duodenum. This overacidity resulted in a burning sensation about thirty minutes after a meal. Jane had learned that eating relieves the pain. More eating, more acid. More stress, more acid. She was given alkaline supplements to control the burning, but, more importantly, she was also taught how to deal with stress. In two months she effortlessly lost 20 pounds. The mind affects the body and the body affects the mind.

Stress

Biochemical changes due to stress can make the victim so uncomfortable that he or she must eat in order to feel better. This may be the principal reason why people abandon diets. They lose weight so long as they stay away from even smelling a favorite food; but when they eat sugar or an allergen, the blood sugar rises, and when it subsequently falls, self-control goes and they blow the diet.

Some observers of the human scene believe that stress is more prevalent in our modern world because of the frustrations we encounter almost daily. One such frustration might occur when we are cornered in a situation in which we feel the need to be cheerful and compliant. For our ancestors, it was simple. Either they ran away from those saber-toothed tigers or they fought them. We must hang around with clenched teeth, keeping the battle within ourselves.

A stress is any change in the external or internal environment that causes a physical or mental response. Small stresses are barely perceptible; you walk uphill and your heart beats faster. But if a stimulus makes you feel uncomfortable, it would be a distress. Exercise is a stress, but it is good for us. Lying in bed would seem like a good way to avoid stress, but while we are thus inactive the body loses calcium, and that is a stress.

We are all different in the way we perceive the stresses in our environment. If your boss or spouse or teacher puts you down and the next day you have a headache, you would acknowledge that you had experienced stress; a friend or co-worker in the same confrontation might get diarrhea. Many do not even notice that they are in a situation of stress, but it is subtly working on them. A person might get used to driving in rush-hour traffic, but it is a stress nonetheless. I would assume that not all of us could stand the noise, confusion, bad odors, and pressures that alternate with the long, boring waits that are part of the life of a cab driver. Some love the job; some hate it. This difference must be due to different perceptions of stress.

We experience stress when a message gets through to the neocortex of the brain that something is impinging on the sensibilities: a reaction of some kind then takes place. The form of the reaction is determined by genetics (eczema, headaches, indigestion, hostility, or obesity). They are all merely symptoms that the homeostasis of the body was disrupted.[5]

There are several ways to counteract stress. We can get out of the stressful situation; we can prepare our nervous system so that it notices the stress less; and we can eat and exercise so prudently that the body is less responsive and homeostasis is more easily maintained.

5. Homeostasis is the condition of optimum function of all the body parts, individually and collectively: muscles, glands, brain, heart, liver, etc. Every injury, twist, insult, temperature change—that is, every stress—sets up a variety of compensating functions to return the body to optimum function. Homeostasis is the physiological/biochemical process by which the body attempts to maintain the neutral or resting phase. If the blood sugar rises, insulin is secreted to lower it. If the foot steps on a tack, the brain notices pain and sends a message to the leg to lift the stupid foot. The body dislikes change and sets in motion mechanisms necessary to counteract the change and restore balance.

If your doctor gives you a drug to treat your depression (or anxiety or insomnia), he is blocking your perception of the stress; remember, however, that the drugs themselves are stressful to the physiology of the body. Our perception of the world might be comfort, but the distress is still in there hurting the liver or kidneys or brain. We must stop just treating the symptoms and do something to help the body maintain homeostasis.

A carpenter, a big muscular type, developed a peptic ulcer mainly because his boss would stand over him, criticizing his work. The carpenter couldn't do anything quite right. He wanted to deck his boss, but felt he might lose his job. His smart therapist tried a reframing method that detoured the stress pathway. The therapist asked if the boss was a better carpenter.

"Sure, but . . ." he admitted.

"Okay," responded the therapist, "the next time he complains about your work, tell him, 'Gee, boss, you do this so well, why don't you teach me how to be as good as you are? Show me how you do it.' You are going to have to swallow your pride, but it will heal the hole in your stomach."

It worked. The internalized battle was eliminated. The carpenter now saw that he had choices. Ten thousand years ago the carpenter probably would not have internalized his frustration and hostility; he probably would have killed the boss. Maybe in the "good ole days" physical labor would have allowed someone with stress to "work it out." But the average life span centuries ago was but twenty-five years, so a person had little chance to get a disease from the stresses that he or she faced on all sides. We all live longer now, and so we are able to see the effects of stress over the long term.

The illnesses and conditions of our ancestors often indicate which organ or system will deteriorate or fail to function if and when stress tilts the homeostasis. The potential organ weakness is carried genetically. The carpenter with the ulcer "due to" a domineering boss probably has a relative with ulcers. The genetic tendency is there, ready to exert its influence or tell the stress which organ to impact. It is obviously multifactoral. Several organs, or even entire body systems, may be affected. My wife and I have had some friends who developed cancer at an early age. Looking back, we realized that these people had suffered excessive stress—constant, unrelenting, inescapable, and long-lasting. It is as if the cancer had come along to get them out of intolerable situations. Someone else similarly stressed might have gotten high blood pressure.

Certain body types seem disposed to suffer in predictable ways. The long, thin, asthenic build is more commonly associated with schizophrenia. The more stolid mesomorph seems prone to manic-depressive psychosis. I have noticed a greater incidence of hyperactivity in blue-eyed blond boys whose families have a higher than average incidence of obesity, diabetes, and alcoholism. Allergists know that allergies are more prominent in the blonds, and especially in freckle-faced, green-eyed redheads. Fair folk must be aware that food allergies play a role in their tendency to obesity. Obesiy is high among the American Indians, along with diabetes and alcoholism. The problem that befalls the individual may be genetically, or congenitally, determined, but the *reason* it happens is stress—emotional, physical, or dietary. The common pathway seems to be that the blood sugar falls, and the adrenals, pancreas, thymus, and liver are burdened to readjust the homeostasis. If the stress is chronic, and if the body is not supplied with the proper nutrients to help the readjustment, some disease, or at least a symptom, will develop.

Fortunately, we have learned a lot about stress in the twenty-eight years since Dr. Hans Selye wrote his pioneering book, *The Stress of Life* (1956). We have enough evidence to help people handle stress better, or to become less distressed by it, and even to protect the target organ from the devastation of the stress.

It seems a sad fact that many people are trying to lose weight on diets that trigger their allergies and exacerbate the stresses in their lives. All they come out with is a net gain in discouragement. But how are they to know? Who is supposed to tell them?

We are all different, and the job of figuring out our physiology is up to each one of us. From the foregoing, you know the questions to ask in building your own profile: about your genetic predispositions, your mother's pregnancy with you, your crucial first year of life, any childhood tendency to overweight, any evidence of absorption problems, the extent to which you may have learned to equate food with emotional comfort, and any stresses that may be taking a toll on you. (Chapters 6 through 8 will give you further insight into stress management.)

Any and all of these factors can distort our physiology, and in this sense each and every one of them is a stress. I believe, therefore, that the key to successful weight management is to arrive at a diet and exercise plan that disarms the stresses in our lives, that helps us get things sparking in a positive direction instead of in the vicious cycle from bad to worse. We have to be healthy to be healthy.

2

The Biochemistry of Weight Control

Why is it, with so many weight control programs in existence, that so many of the people who try them slip back into their rolls of fat as if nothing had happened? Are they genetically destined always to carry this extra weight? Are they programmed emotionally as infants to eat everything in sight when they meet any frustration? Do they have a lesion in their hypothalamus that neurologically prevents them from receiving and responding to messages from the stomach and blood chemicals?

Many already know what is preventing their success: They eat sugar, white flour products, foods full of fat, and foods that are calorically dense.[1] Their exercise consists of getting up in

1. According to a study by the Health Insurance Association of America, we have changed our dietary habits greatly in the last century. We eat 34 percent more fat than we did in 1900 and 17 percent fewer carbohydrates. We are eating more canned and frozen foods and fewer fresh fruits. We eat more meat than in 1900; poultry consumption has risen, but beef and veal sales are down.

the morning and getting dressed; they stand on the down escalator. They feel so tired because of the rotten diet that they cannot exercise, which in itself would make their blood flow and relieve their fatigue.

Some tired, discouraged, and overweight folk hope that an endocrine dysfunction is the reason for their problem; and that a simple, appropriate pill will remove the excess weight. Neurological hurts to the appetite control center of the hypothalamus probably explain only about one out of ten thousand cases of obesity, but the temporary inactivity of the thyroid appears to be a fairly common reason for insignificant weight loss in response to a low-calorie diet.

Weight gain occurring simultaneously with aging is usually blamed on the loss of efficiency of the older muscles in burning up fat. Older people find they must eat less and exercise more just to maintain their ideal weight.

But maybe you already know these things. You are asking what new information research has provided to help us take care of ourselves. Is it possible to turn the switch from "store" to "burn" when we swallow food? Can we become more efficient despite genetic and lifestyle insurmountables? Can we make the enzymes, determined by the genes, more active by using supplements? What's going on at the cellular level?

Research on animals and humans in the last decade has revealed facts of great importance for weight management:

• The mind affects the body and the body affects the mind, and some parts of the mind affect other parts of the mind.

• Weight management is more than just a formula (calories taken in; equal calories expended).

• We are all different.

First, however, we should review the calorie theory of weight control. It says that ingested food becomes chemical energy. If more energy is taken in than is used up in the work of the body, the excess will be stored in the tissues or excreted in the feces.

Part of the energy used is for the basal metabolic rate. This is the hum of life's machinery at the molecular level. It is what keeps our temperature at 98° to 98.6°. The energy to maintain this is being lost continually. The amount of heat produced depends on the volume of the individual, while the amount of heat lost depends on the surface area (total square inches of skin). Elephants and whales lose a smaller fraction of their total energy as heat than do small rodents, for example. Small mammals must eat a relatively large amount of food to maintain correct body temperature and keep up with energy requirements. They burn a lot of calories foraging for food to get enough energy to forage for food. As dieters lose weight, therefore, losing should be easier, because a higher percentage of the energy taken in is lost as heat.

Ingested energy is burned up by the working muscles, by the brain (one of the busiest organs), and by each cell of the body. But much energy is lost through the feces. Our bodies are not efficient machines for the absorption of utilizable energy from the food swallowed. Fecal material has about the same energy potential per unit mass of dry weight as the ingested fuel. (Remember buffalo chips? Some people of India cook their food by burning the dried chips of the sacred cows.)

Much research has been focused on *why* we eat in the first place. Communication networks involving nerves and circulating chemicals are required to tell us when to *start* eating, as well as when to stop. The hypothalamus, deep in the brain, is the chief and central regulator of activities designed either to get food (forage) or to stop swallowing because one feels full. The ventromedial area of the hypothalamus is called the satiety center, or appestat, because when this part is stimulated, the owner will stop eating. Certain biochemical events are associated with stimulation of the ventromedial area: less stomach acid is produced and less insulin is released from the pancreas. Stimulation of the cluster of nerve cells just lateral to this area results in feeding activity plus insulin release and acid secretion in the stomach. But it would not be accurate to say that the human has only two responses, depending on which area of the hypothalamus is stimulated.

Years ago, when these two centers were discovered, it was felt that they were responsive only to blood sugar fluctuations. (Blood sugar falls: Start eating because the lateral hypothalamus has alerted the whole body to forage. Blood sugar rises: The ventromedial area tells the mouth to quit.) Now investigators have found other modifying nerve connections and chemicals. For instance, the ventromedial center is associated with a pathway that utilizes serotonin as a transmitter. Carbohydrate bingers may be trying to make enough serotonin to stimulate the satiety center; then they can quit. They have to consume fairly good-sized loads of carbohydrates to get a surge of serotonin to turn off their hunger. If these people are placed on a protein-rich diet, the serotonin precursor (tryptophan) is competitively excluded from reaching the brain by the other amino acids. So the serotonin-sensitive appestat is unsatisfied, and these dieters might feel awful—or at least stressed—until they get their sugar-starch load again. It's called binging. (It is possible that this subgroup of carbo-snackers might do well to take a pill of tryptophan (500 mg) in the late afternoon or evening to curb the lust for the high-calorie snack often needed at bedtime.)

Dopamine is another neurotransmitter that affects nerve transmission in the hypothalamus. Widely separated areas of the brain have nerve connections to these hypothalamic areas. (Why do you salivate when you smell a bakery?)[2] Glucose levels of the blood do have an effect on eating activity, but so do fatty acids. These are prostaglandin precursors and tend to suppress eating. Purines will suppress the appetite also; maybe eating a little meat and fat at the beginning of the meal might kill your appetite for dessert. Try it.

Peptides, or chains of amino acids, act as regulators. Cho-

2. The serotonin- and dopamine-sensitive tracts are associated with the pleasure center of the brain.

lecystokinin (CCK) is released from the duodenum when long-chain fatty acids, amino acids, and calcium are ingested. This CCK delays stomach-emptying, and thus helps suppress the appetite. The vagus nerve, which runs from the brain to the stomach and intestines, has the receptors for CCK, which would then activate the ventromedial (satiety) area of the hypothalamus.

Bombesin, another peptide, is liberated during eating and has an anorectic (appetite suppressing) effect. Calcitonin from the thyroid gland cuts eating activities. CRF, or corticotropin-releasing factor (a peptide), slows the appetite. It is secreted during stress and releases adrenocorticotrophic hormone (ACTH), thus stimulating the adrenals. This brain-adrenal connection is overactive in anorexia patients.

Phenylalanine can act as an appetite suppressant; 500 mg is the usual dose. It is supposed to aid in the formation of catecholamines.[3] It could also compete with tryptophan and interfere with the production of serotonin.

Research has discovered endogenous opiates in our brains. These are peptides called endorphins. They may turn out to be the driving force that makes us eat. Animals given morphinelike substances into their brains will eat. Naloxone, a morphine antagonist, suppresses food intake in obese humans. Hurting or stressing animals will induce feeding activity; the endorphins produced with painful stimuli encourage foraging behavior.[4]

Because so many theories have been advanced to explain nutrient control of food intake (glucose, fatty acids, energy foods, minerals, and amino acids), it may mean the brain contains mechanisms to regulate the levels of all essential nutrients. If you are thirsty, the brain makes you seek fluid. If you are low in zinc, your brain makes you seek out zinc-bearing foods. If your blood

3. Catecholamines (like adrenalin) suppress the appetite. But dl-phenylalanine will slow an enzyme that metabolizes endorphins.
4. John Merky, M.B., and Allen S. Levine, Ph.D., "Central Control of Appetite," *Lancet*, 19 February 1983.

sugar is low, your body will crave sugary foods. Do criminals crave milk because they need calcium or because they are addicted to milk? Do chocolate lovers have a need for chocolate or do they crave the magnesium that is in chocolate? If you get too many calories in your search for all the nutrients you need and you gain weight, it suggests you are eating too many calorie-dense (nutrient-poor) foods

In 1928 Dr. Clara M. Davis, a pediatrician, fed seven- to nine-month-old infants a number of wholesome, mostly natural foods. In a week they were all happily and compliantly eating a balanced diet. (If sugar and white flour had been served, about 20 percent of the children would still be eating those nonfoods.)[5] It seems, then, that before we are seduced by the sugar, salt, and fat in the nutrient-poor, calorie-rich foods of the American diet, we humans *do* have the innate sense to choose a balanced diet without being taught. But we, like Dr. Davis's babies, must be *exposed to a variety of wholesome foods.*

EXERCISE, THE ESSENTIAL FACTOR

In theory, we are supposed to lose weight if we eat less than the body's metabolic rate requires. The basic flaw in the theory is that it doesn't work. To repeat, if the caloric intake is reduced to below that of the body's metabolic rate, the body will dampen down the fires and reduce its metabolic rate. When the body is deprived of the energy it needs for functioning, it can reduce its rate 10 to 45 percent through the adjustment of hormones and enzymes.[6]

5. Clara M. Davis, M.D., "Self-Selection of Diet by Newly Weaned Infants," *American Journal of Diseases of Children* 36 (1928), pp. 651–679.

6. In a human metabolic study reported in the *Journal of the American Medical Association*, vol. 237, no. 26 (27 June 1977), p. 2831, nine persons did not lose on a 1000-calorie diet. They had substantially lower oxygen consumption rates than others and greater than average numbers of fat storage cells. The article concluded that some obese people are metabolically adapted to an efficient use of a small amount of food.

When deprived of carbohydrate fuel, the body begins to use protein. Muscle mass, or lean body tissue, disappears. Endurance and strength are sapped. Weakness, irritability, headaches, and constipation all follow, and the frustrated dieter abandons restraint and becomes a nervous predator. Anything not nailed down goes into the mouth. The sweeter the better. Fat stores balloon.

Exercise is the factor that can change all this. Exercise will keep the metabolic rate from dropping when caloric intake is reduced. Exercise keeps the hormonal and enzyme systems stimulated and increases the muscle mass; wasting will not occur. Ingestion of complex carbohydrates will provide the fuel for energy, thus sparing the muscle tissue itself. After exercise, fat is liberated from the storage depots. Without exercise, weight loss is practically impossible if one is to remain healthy at the same time. New habits must last a lifetime.

Tiny structures in body cells, called mitochondria, are responsible for energy conversion from fat. Exercise increases the work of the mitochrondria by a factor of 3. But when one feels so tired, how does one get out the door and at least walk around the block?

There is help and hope ahead. Hang in there. If we know something about the biochemical mechanism, we may be able to change our lifestyle accordingly. Knowledge may lead to insight and provide the incentive to try again.

The word *aerobic*, which we hear mostly in connection with exercise, refers to oxygen. Aerobic metabolism is the process the body uses to burn fat; its end products are water and carbon dioxide. Aerobic exercise is exercise done while there is adequate oxygen in the tissues. If not enough oxygen is present in the body while fuel is burned, the result is *anaerobic* metabolism. The end products of this inefficient type of combustion are pyruvate and lactate, which build up in the tissues, leading to sore muscles, wasting of trace minerals, and some loss of nervous-system function.

In order to attain an oxygen-efficient level of metabolism, we have to exercise strenuously enough to raise the heartbeat to an estimated 70 percent of its maximum for our particular age. (Some individuals, due to a genetic block, are unable to achieve efficient use of oxygen, however.)

The increase of the mitochondria in the cells and their enzyme systems will convert anaerobic metabolism to the efficient aerobic type. The mitochondria allow the fat energy to be burned instead of stored. Exercise is what causes this conversion to take place, but motivation to exercise is difficult because of the fatigue.

A doctor looking you in the eye and demanding your involvement in a planned program is one source of motivation. Another is the boss (or the colonel) telling you that you're fired (or discharged) if you don't start working out at least every couple of days. A boyfriend or girlfriend or new spouse might help one turn the corner.

I am disturbed that everyone's family doctor (or any doctor or naturopath or chiropractor or psychologist) does not routinely dog his or her patients to move. Your dentist would be remiss if he didn't hold the drill over your open tooth cavity and say, "Do you promise to stop eating junk? Do you swear you will exercise and take calcium and magnesium?"

The height/weight proportion is still a pretty good clue to nutrition. Insurance companies could do a lot more to motivate their clients if they shot up the premium for people whose lifestyle includes overweight, smoking, and lack of exercise.

Diet pills may give some appetite suppression, but have proved to be but a temporary bandage. Exercise and lifestyle changes must be made to produce long term results. Obese people tend to have an increase in their blood pressure and many of the diet pills will aggravate that tendency.

The American College of Sports Medicine has made the following recommendations for the development and maintenance of optimum cardiorespiratory fitness:

1. Training should be three to five times a week.

2. Duration should be fifteen to sixty minutes, depending upon the type of activity.

3. The elevated heart rate (180 minus the age in years) should be maintained for about twelve minutes. For another way to determine the desired pulse during exercise, figure 220 minus your age; then take 75 percent of that. I am sixty-two, so my formula is $220 - 62 = 158; 0.75 \times 158 = 118$ beats per minute. As you improve your strength and endurance, you might increase the pulse by ten to twenty beats per minute, but start with the following:

Age	Optimum exercise pulse rate (in beats per minute)
up to 25	140–175
26–35	130–170
36–40	120–160
41–45	120–155
46–50	115–150
51–55	110–145
56 on	110–140

4. The activity should be aerobic. It should use large muscle groups on a continuous basis in a rhythmical fashion, such as running, jogging, walking or hiking, swimming, bicycling, ropeskipping.

5. You should increase the exercise gradually. Walking around the block is a start. The marathon is later. The heart rate needs to be increased and it should be sustained for fifteen to sixty minutes. If you exercise less than three times a week, it is difficult to improve your metabolism. The following should help:

Exercise	Calories burned (per hour)	Time required
Walking	300	45 min. 3×/week
Running	630	30 min. 3×/week

Exercise	Calories burned (per hour)	Time required
Swimming	650	30 min. 3×/week
Bicycling	660	30 min. 3×/week
Tennis	480	30 min. 3×/week
Cross-country skiing	540	30 min. 3×/week
Horseback riding	345	60 min. 2×/week
Aerobic dancing	480	30 min. 3×/week

6. Before exercising, stretch the major muscles you will be using during the exercise. This warm-up is important, since the muscles can be injured easily if one plunges right into heavy exercise. Cool down slowly afterward. Avoid getting chilled.

Somehow you have to make it fun. Exercising with friends or in a class helps.

If a person has been heavy since birth, it would be unfair to label that person uncooperative if he or she could not get to the ideal weight for height listed in the Metropolitan Life Insurance Company tables (see page 4). However, if a heavy person has high blood pressure, diabetes, or hyperlipidemia, a more aggressive attempt at weight loss should be launched. If those risk factors are present and the weight is at the upper limits of "normal," weight loss would be prudent.

Those who have been and are still morbidly obese (that is, at least 100 pounds over the ideal) should aim to reduce at least to the point of losing these risk factors. These people may never be able to get into the ideal range. Their physicians should not make them feel guilty, since further weight loss may not be beneficial to health.

The lean, perhaps even scrawny types who cannot seem to gain on any diet might be suffering from a malabsorption problem. Those vitamin B shots, including B_{12} and folic acid, might be tried for a few weeks to help the digestive enzymes do their job. But forced weight gain is not a goal, since it might trigger metabolic abnormalities such as increased size of fat cells, insulin resistance, hyperlipidemia, and even diabetes.

Ethan Simms, M.D., Professor of Medicine at the University of Vermont, also feels that different types of obesity should be treated in different ways. "Lifelong obesity may carry less of a risk than gaining weight in adult life. Late gainers seem to have a larger share of kidney, heart disease and hypertension problems."[7]

The message here is that one should get oneself into the hands of a thoughtful and sympathetic health facilitator who will monitor the weight, blood pressure, blood tests, and lifestyle so that small symptoms will not coalesce and become big diseases. The doctor—or other health facilitator (*see* Chapter 9)—and the patient should arrive at a goal that is ideal for the patient, based on family history, childhood weight, and any associated risk factors.

If a patient has established a good relationship over the years with his or her doctor and has begun to get middle-age spread, it should be fairly easy for the doctor to motivate the patient to dump those love handles. Blood tests may help goad the patient into a better diet-lifestyle formula. High triglycerides (greater than 150 mg per cent) and a cholesterol rate higher than 230 mg per cent in the serum may have special clout in turning the patient around. With some, it may be necessary to resolve psychological problems or find better ways to cope with stress before weight loss can be achieved.

There is hope ahead. Inching oneself into health will have rewards, albeit slowly realized. Every nutritional improvement and lifestyle change takes at least a month to produce measurable benefits in energy increase, weight decrease, and mental outlook. As my friend Larry Grant observes, the call for instant nutritional resurrection is almost never heeded; the goal should be a gradual yet steady transition to healthy living through the ingestion of wholesome food and a prudent exercise program.

7. Reported in the *Journal of the American Medical Association*, vol. 239, no. 17 (28 April 1978), p. 1727.

3

The Diet Derby

If you have ever been to a weight loss clinic or read some books on the subject, you have probably seen the following diet or something like it a few times. It's the Usual Basic Boring Diet, and it should work if you are reasonably normal. But you are reading this book because you suspect that you are *not* reasonably normal. On paper the diet looks effective, but in practice it is loaded with faults, and just glancing at it may make you nauseated. It looks pretty much like this:

BREAKFAST
2 eggs, soft-boiled or poached, with vegetable salt
2 carrot sticks, ¼ green pepper, 1 celery stalk, ⅙ of a
    cucumber for chewing pleasure
8 ounces of nonfat milk

MIDMORNING SNACK
Hard-boiled egg, *or*
4 tablespoons low-fat cottage cheese, *or*

1 cup amino acid drink
Raw vegetables, romaine lettuce, green onion

LUNCH

6 ounces of cottage cheese, *or*
3 ounces of tuna fish, water-packed
Salad, and vegetable chewies

MIDAFTERNOON SNACK

Another cup of amino acid drink

EVENING MEAL

4 to 6 ounces of lean meat, fish, or poultry, broiled or
    baked
1 or 2 steamed or barely cooked vegetables
A generous salad
Fruit for dessert
Some caffeine-free herb tea (to help take your mind off
    your evening distress), with ½ teaspoon of honey
    as sweetener (optional)

This turns out to be about 70 grams of protein and about
1000 to 1200 calories for the day. It provides the needed calcium,
roughage, and—if you used a little salad oil—the fatty acids. It
is fairly well balanced; there should be no serious deprivations
on this diet.

It is a standard regime, but it might prove worthless because
no reasonably normal person would tolerate it for more than
three days. Its real problem is that it would tend to promote
allergies because of its reliance on amino acid drinks (soy and
dairy protein) and on milk and cottage cheese. I would be constipated and have a chronic bloody nose on this diet. (Dr. Shirley
Lorenzani at the Page Clinic in Saint Petersburg Beach, Florida,
makes the point that milk upsets the mineral ratios in the blood
of most people.)

A weight-control diet has to be sane enough that a dieter can stick with it and stay healthy. The diet should allow for loss of fat from fat stores without jeopardizing lean muscle tissue. I was surprised and saddened to learn that a fast—just water and no food—would indeed take weight off the fasting person, but 35 percent would be removed from the fat stores, and the remaining 65 percent would be dropped from the muscles. A diet that concentrates on burning fat can lead to dangerous levels of ketones in the blood. If a diet does not stabilize the blood sugar at a level compatible with comfort and brain function, the dieter will feel awful and will probably abandon the regime. A diet that uses only one or a few foods often leads to food sensitivities and consequent hypoglycemia and dyspepsia. The foods provided should be adequate in vitamins, amino acids, fatty acids, minerals, and fiber for that particular dieter. They should promote bowel movements that are soft in consistency and occur at least daily, if not more frequently. Supplementation may be required.

The problem with most of the recently promoted diets is that they are too one-sided. Perhaps the authors have had luck with certain patients or clients and then assumed by extrapolation that their diets will work for everyone.

The *Beverly Hills Diet* is too high in sugar and too low in protein. It is low in foods that commonly trigger allergies (hypoallergenic), and thus there may be some initial weight loss due to the loss of edema fluid that often accumulates when people eat foods to which they are sensitive. Judy Mazel has some worthwhile suggestions—like sequencing foods, combining foods, and warning about the problems of milk intolerance[1]—but the diet is very low in protein, allows muscle wasting to occur, and because of the high sugar content leads to the production of triglycerides.

The *Beverly Hills Medical Diet* by Dr. Arnold Fox seems more logical, safe, and appropriate. Most people would be com-

1. Judy Mazel, *The Beverly Hills Diet* (St. Louis Park, Minn.: Chain-Pinkham Books, 1981).

fortable with this and might stick with it for a long time. But it does not go far enough.

Dr. Robert Atkins' *Super Energy Diet* is high in protein and fat and is based on the idea that if the blood sugar can be kept at a safe, even level, there will be no hypoglycemia to trigger the impulse to eat. This diet produces high levels of ketones, a condition that causes acidosis and anorexia; ketosis can be dangerous to some people. Calcium and magnesium are lost through the urine in this high-protein (high-phosphorus) diet. Trace minerals run out of the body and muscle enzymes are depleted.

Protein-sparing modified diets are based on the concept that if a good balance of amino acid protein source is taken, the muscles will be spared during the calorie reduction. The weight loss will be at the expense of the fat, not of the muscle. The *Cambridge Diet* product had soy and milk protein to which many people are very sensitive. Drinking this daily could lead to a weight gain and not a loss. Many of these protein drink diets are not balanced in their mineral and vitamin content, and many are heavily sweetened and colored with artificial materials. The allergies produced may not be worth the promised fat loss.

Collagen-based protein products (fortunately not widely available anymore) are poorly absorbed and could lead to malnutrition if used more than just occasionally. The low amount of potassium and the nutritionally deficient protein in these drinks lead to fatal cardiac arrhythmias in some people. A low-calorie diet should be supplemented with essential elements, vitamins, and minerals to be safe. The body cannot do its work without the proper enzymes, and these need their vitamin and mineral precursors.[2]

The *Save Your Life Diet* put forward by Dr. David Reuben approaches the primitive diet because of the emphasis on fiber. The author does not restrict calories, but allows the dieter to

2. J. M. Amatruda, M.D., "Vigorous supplementation," *American Journal of Medicine* 74 (June 1983), p. 1016.

fill up on bran, water, raw vegetables, and whole grains, and, of course, he forbids the use of sugar and white-flour products. The distention of the stomach from the fiber and roughage acts as the limiting factor to eating. It makes some sense, but if one is sensitive to wheat and grains, it could be disastrous.

The *Zen macrobiotic diet* is basically a well-balanced vegetarian diet, but it progresses into a limited, extremely deficient brown rice intake only. If adhered to, it leads to scurvy, anemia, hypocalcemia, and hypoproteinemia. Ohsawa's *Macrobiotics* has generally been disavowed by Zen Buddhists.

The *Scarsdale Diet* is a rigid two-week diet high in protein and low in carbohydrate. It could do what it claims to do in the two weeks, but there is little guidance for the years afterwards. It has more than 35 percent fat and is low in calcium and magnesium. The maintenance diet after the fourteen-day regime requires a Spartan determination.

Nathan Pritikin saved his own life some years ago when he researched the best method of cleaning out his sludged blood vessels. His Longevity Center in Santa Barbara advocates a very low fat intake (less than 10 percent), no refined sugar, 80 percent complex carbohydrate, and about 10 percent protein. The Pritikin Diet may be low in calcium, iron, and B_{12}, but adherents have been able to lose weight (it's about 1000 calories a day) and, best of all, they exhibit a very low incidence of heart attacks and reduced need for heart bypass surgery for angina, and in some cases have eliminated mature-onset diabetes. Exercise is increased slowly to tolerance.

Pritikin allows meat in the diet, but keeps it close to $3\frac{1}{2}$ ounces a day; he is afraid that if he eliminated animal meat from the diet entirely he would have too many defectors from the plan. He also feels that strict vegetarians do not need to balance the amino acids at each meal (such as beans with grains); if they get some variety over the course of a few days, they will get a balance. He feels that most of us eat too much meat protein anyway. Meat, remember, tends to push calcium out of the bones. (Vegetarians lose only about half the calcium that is lost from the bones of meat-eating adults.) Pritikin also believes that his diet does not need vitamin supplementation.

Weight Watchers have an effective and realistic diet that aims for a modest 1- to 2-pound loss per week. Group-support therapy is built into the program. It might be low in vitamin E, iron, and magnesium.

The *Diet Center Diet* is high in protein and fat and recommends calcium supplements since milk intake is restricted. The *Weight Loss Clinic* uses a high-protein diet and supplements to supply the unmet needs.[3] The concept of each diet, whether it uses protein or complex carbohydrates, is to keep the blood sugar at such a level that the brain is nourished and temptations are minimized. If the foraging center in the hypothalamus gets a chemical message, it will respond: once food searching begins, it rarely stops until food gets to the stomach. Many people are discouraged with all these diets because of the monotony and the gas.

Dr. Broda Barnes[4] feels that "an effective diet and good thyroid function" will normalize about everyone. He believes the mistake of most diet plans is the reliance on low fat intake— assuming that "fat is the larding factor." He learned from farmers that when animals are to be fattened for market, fat is eliminated from their diets and cereals are shoveled in. These seem to create a high blood sugar level and a consequent release of insulin which drives the sugar into the fat cells and stimulates the liver to make triglycerides. If fat is put in the diet, the stomach empties very slowly and there is no sudden rise in the blood sugar; the dieter (or hog) feels full and stops eating. This method takes longer to get the ham and the beef fattened and ready for the

3. R. B. Friedman, M.D., et al., "Weight Loss Methods," *Post Graduate Medicine* 72 (October 1982), pp. 73–76.

4. *Hypothyroidism: The Unsuspected Illness* (New York: Thomas Y. Crowell, 1976).

market place, so the farmers often fatten the animals on corn instead.

Dr. Barnes's suggestion for a 1300-calorie-per-day diet has 50 grams of carbohydrate, 70 grams of protein, and—get this—90 grams of fat. He had many patients who lost weight on this. He also found that patients on a low-fat, high-protein, and moderate-carbohydrate diet developed hypothyroidism as evidenced by fatigue, a sensation of coldness, and an elevated serum cholesterol. They needed 4 grains of thyroid extract (desiccated) to handle the extra protein in their high-protein diet.

Ms. Diane Broughton in her *Thumper Newsletter*[5] has researched the vegetarian-versus-carnivore controversy and believes that the dieters who have problems are the meat-eaters. After Ms. Broughton quoted Nathan Pritikin to the effect that the Atkins diet was life-threatening because it led to heart attacks and diabetes, Dr. Atkins brought suit for libel. He dropped his suit, however, after he was forced to admit that his own records showed a correlation between his high-meat diet and a high incidence of heart attacks and diabetes. Nathan Pritikin's diet helps prevent these diseases and allows for weight management and maintenance.

Those meat-eaters who developed cardiovascular difficulties may not have been paying attention to their thyroid function; cholesterol rises when the thyroid sleeps. Perhaps thyroid medication should accompany the high-protein diet prescription. Or perhaps meat-eaters should also eat the animals' thyroid gland.

Ms. Broughton summarizes the approach that should work on all (or most all) of us: "The foods to remember: fresh fruits and vegetables, whole grains, brown rice and fish." She reminds us that eighty years ago doctors tried to alert us to eat our diseases away: fresh fruits and vegetables, whole grains, some fish, skim or acidophilus milk.

5. Broughton Press, P.O. Box 36C96, Los Angeles, CA 90036.

Mr. Pritikin does not favor avocados, seeds, or nuts because of their rather high fat content. (Chestnuts are okay.) This may be the chief reason for noncompliance with Pritikin's longevity diet: it is largely limited to nonfatty foods—but, unfortunately for Pritikin adherents, it is the fat in foods that provides the flavor. Pritikin feels that fat in the diet is destructive; he limits protein intake to 10 percent of the diet. He, too, would have you feel full with fruits, vegetables, whole grains, and a little broiled fish. These are full of nutrients, fiber, and bulk; the distended stomach is the message to the thalamus that stops the foraging. If you have been eating empty calories for a while, your body may be starved for the vitamins and minerals in these nutrient-dense foods. If you still crave carbohydrates, your body may be trying to get some serotonin manufactured so you can be calm.

In all fairness, it must be added that Pritikin has jazzed up his recipes to imitate—in taste only—the high-fat, high-sugar diet of most of the eaters in the United States. I assume, however, that if one has good cause to be motivated—rolling obesity, the threat of the cardiac surgeon's knife, or the gangrene of diabetes—one would start eating those "foods to remember."

So it looks like you have some choices. But you need some help—the diet itself is not enough. You need to study your ancestry, and get an exam from the doctor which includes blood tests. You also have to be prepared to try different approaches. Remember, we are all different. The key questions—which the diet authors don't ask and which your doctor *should* ask—are, "Are you in pain? Are you experiencing stress?" If there is stress, it may be encouraging the formation of endorphins and *that* could be making you eat.

You can expect to fail in any attempt at weight control unless the program has balance built into it. There have to be nutritious foods, taken in the right amounts at the right times and in the right sequence.

There has to be a balanced array of nutritional supports, because when intake is reduced the metabolism, helping us to survive "in time of famine," starts using up the body's stores of vitamins and minerals. Supplements also help to keep the stresses in our lives at manageable levels of perception.

A diet should not throw the body chemically out of balance by producing toxic by-products or triggering allergies.

A diet must also go hand in hand with a balanced lifestyle—which may mean exercising if we don't already do it, and getting our addictions (coffee, booze, cigarettes) under control. Some pin their hopes on diet pills. While these preparations may suppress the appetite to some extent, they cannot substitute for exercise and lifestyle changes. Unfortunately, some of these pills contain ingredients that aggravate the tendency to high blood pressure, a condition common in overweight people.

Most of all, a diet only works when it is undertaken with balanced mental outlook. The dieter must accept that it is going to take time. Indeed, gradualism seems to be the only way to capture the minds and stomachs of the plump ones on our planet. When heavy folk decide to shuck their extra pounds, they frequently expect to go on a diet and drop ten "big ones" in a week. They have set their goals at a ridiculously high level and are bound to be disappointed. They feel depressed and trapped; they feel they have lost control, which is a stress that can make them gain again—and faster. Follow-up studies of participants on weight control programs reveal that 70 to 90 percent are back to their preprogram weights in just nine to twelve months.

The trap seems to be in the idea of "going on" and "going off" a diet. That's exactly what happens. The "crash" in crash diets comes afterward, when we start gobbling food to assuage the demands of our depleted bodies. Instead, the diet we follow for weight reduction should be the comfortable, just-right diet we can follow for the rest of our lives without boredom. Scots might find that scones, oatmeal, haggis, and applesauce would be important items in the diet. Germans would get the cabbage and potatoes and pork in there. A person with Greek blood running through her veins might notice contentment and ease of acceptance with olive oil on the salad, whole grains, goat's milk, and fresh fruit and vegetables and maybe a dollop of honey occasionally. We are all truly different, and one man's nectar may be another's poison. But there *are* some basic rules to follow.

4

Can You Swing If You're Fat?

It should be firmly established in your head now that the best way to preserve your sanity in a world gone mad, to maintain an ideal weight for your frame (plus or minus 10 pounds), and to achieve the potential your genes have promised, is to eat foods that your body can assimilate for energy, that provide for repair, that bolster your immune system, and that are least likely to cause allergic reactions.

When you eat food that your body is constructed to eat, you will lose the symptom: poor weight control. You might find it worthwhile simply to disregard the whole narrow, boring, restrictive, tiresome, frustrating concept of dieting. Instead, aim for optimum health: the weight will then take care of itself.

The next chapter sets forth what I call *Dr. Smith's Low-Stress Weight Control Diet* (a diet, it seems, must have a name). It is a natural, nongimmicky diet that provides for everything required for health. If you feel good on this diet, exercise moderately, surround yourself with interesting work or entertaining alternatives and supportive friends, the symptom of weight dys-control will disappear. Homeostasis is the goal, and diet can allow it to happen.

Our body's biochemical functions are programmed to work efficiently and exactly if given the proper amounts of needed supplies: oxygen, water, protein, fats, carbohydrates, vitamins, and minerals. If we do not follow the rules under which the body/mind is designed to function, we create the potential for a problem. Break the rules, and you will get a symptom. You can't fool Mother Nature. I get headaches; you might gain weight. Your body is telling you, Listen! Put your ear on your bellybutton and listen to the complaints.

But first, in order to manage your weight effectively, there are general rules of eating that need to be incorporated into your life patterns. These are not temporary measures just for the sake of losing a few big ones. They are part of a style of thought and behavior that is to go on from day to day. The body is designed to be so treated. Adopt the following rules, memorize them, and repeat them daily as a sort of daily prayer, a list of dietary commandments.

1. *I will read all labels before I buy any food.* Or, better still, *If a food has a label, I will try not to buy it.* A grocery store manager told me that the healthiest people who come into his store are the Southeast Asians who have not learned to read English yet. They shop around the edges of the store and pick the fish, poultry, fruit, and vegetables. They do buy white rice, but that is about the only processed food they get. The more processed a food, the more likely it is to be empty of nutrients; in just a day or two the eater can expect to see it on his or her waist.

2. *I will eat foods as close as possible to the natural state.* Or, *If God made it, it is probably okay to eat it.* (But remember, God made toadstools, rhubarb leaves, and potato stems.) Natural foods are cheaper, too. A potato is cheaper than

chips or fries. You can buy three loaves of white balloon bread for the price of one whole-grain loaf, but one slice of the latter will fill you up better than the empty-air bread. We have a stone-age intestinal tract, so we should be eating stone-age foods. (Don't try to run naked through the local park eating bark, blossoms, and berries. The police would arrest you and then you would be eating prison food.)

3. *I will eat food as fresh as possible and if it is still moving, so much the better.* If you lived in a cave ten thousand years ago and a mouse scurried by, you might grab it, squeeze it, smash it against the wall, and then eat it whole. (Spit out the tail.) Try to imitate this ancestral behavior. Fresh foods are the best, then frozen, then dried, then canned. Use the quick-fry method (wok) or the steamer for the vegetables. Much of the vitamins and minerals diffuse out in the water when foods are boiled. Potatoes should be cooked, not eaten raw. When eating raw carrots, chew thirty times before swallowing.

4. *I will try to make fruits and vegetables two-thirds of my diet.* You don't have to be a vegan vegetarian, but to approximate that persuasion is a healthy and inexpensive lifestyle. Nathan Pritikin has saved many cardiac cripples from a bypass operation with a diet that has negligible sugar, no fat, and only a little meat. Meat-eaters, in general, get too much phosphorus and suffer the devastation of osteoporosis (bent backs, muscle cramps, easy fractures, and tooth loss). Meat-eaters are more susceptible to gout, colon disease, cancer, and smelly gas. *If I do eat red meat, I will keep it to 4 ounces every week or two.* Even when all the visible fat is cut off the steak, 30 to 50 percent of what's left is fat. It is almost impossible to reduce when eating red meat daily. We need protein—but *lean* protein. *I won't eat the skin.* (Darn it—that's where the flavor is!) Chicken, turkey, lamb, fish. Baked, broiled, roasted. Not fried. Complex carbohydrates (corn, potatoes, brown rice, and whole grains such as oats, barley, whole wheat, and buckwheat) have fiber to keep the sugar from hitting the body all at once. They are digested and absorbed slowly over a three-hour period, producing a slow trickle of glucose into the cells. If there is no excess, nothing gets stored. Fiber provides the bulk that scoots the food through the tortuous tunnels of the intestines.

5. *I will try to avoid white sugar, brown sugar, honey, maple syrup, and molasses.* Here is the continuum from bad to good: white sugar, honey, maple syrup, molasses, refined grains, dried fruit, whole grains, beans, fresh fruit, vegetables, nuts, seeds. *I do not need to salt everything.* Only vegan vegetarians need to salt their food. Zucchini, celery, string beans, and summer squash have sodium. It is sodium chloride (table salt) that we need to use so sparingly.

6. *I will try not to eat the same food every day. Rotating my diet is a way to minimize the chance of developing food allergies.* See if you can limit your coffee, soft drinks, and cola drinks to one every four days! The things you love are the things that may be causing your symptoms. The "good for you" foods often are the ones most likely to cause the sensitivities: milk, soy, corn, wheat, and eggs. Frequent ingestion of *any* food may lead to a sensitivity.

7. *I will avoid eating if I am nervous, angry, upset, depressed, or being screamed at.* Stress ruins the body's ability to digest and absorb the food swallowed. Once when I was looking through a proctoscope at my medical-school partner's colon mucosa, I saw it turn a vivid red. I realized that he had blushed inside. Although he was upside down, he had seen the sheer stockings and high heeled shoes of one of the female medical students who had just wandered in, and he was embarrassed because his toosh was exposed. I'm sure if he had just eaten lunch, his sandwich would have fermented instead of getting digested.

Take a minute to just sit quietly before eating; become aware of how your body feels. Feel the hunger pangs, the rumbling. Get rid of negative thoughts. Take a deep breath and blow it out. Saying grace before a meal seems to rid the brain of anti-digestive thoughts—like erasing the blackboard. The neocortex sends good vibrations to the thalamus and on to the gut. Saying grace out loud will really cut down on the gas. Gratitude and joy improve digestion.

8. *I will eat all the protein on my plate first and then chew the vegetables and grains about thirty times before swallowing.* The stomach acids should not be diluted with water, juice, salad, or sugary foods before these acids have a chance to work on the protein. While the protein is being churned about in the stomach, you should chew up the vegetables until they become soupy in the mouth and then they may be swallowed. If the food is not chewed thoroughly, the stomach and the intestines have to work harder. Lots of chewing will make you feel full and you will stop eating sooner. Sugar interferes with the digestion of meat and this protein is then attacked by bacteria; it putrefies. The toxic end products could cause some disturbing symptoms, plus bad breath and smelly wind.

9. *I will eat slowly, putting my fork or spoon down while chewing. I will observe the food and even assign it to parts of my body that might need it.* If you eat carrots tell them to go to your eyes and your skin where they belong. If you are swallowing some bran or roughage, assign it to your colon, tell it to hold onto some moisture and make your next bowel movement soft and easy. Use a variety of foods to provide color, texture, and smell to enjoy and savor. But talk *to yourself* about the disposition of the food; talking out loud while eating allows you to swallow air and that contributes to intestinal wind.

10. *I will try to eat only when I am hungry, and will try to stop eating before I feel full.* Thin people have a characteristic eating pattern. We can learn from them. They eat only when hungry, and when they are no longer hungry they stop eating, even if there is food on the plate. Some heavies I know need to empty the plate; they can be helped by using smaller plates. Thin people look on eating as just another bodily function, like breathing: no big deal.

When the blood sugar drops, the foraging area of the hypothalamus is activated and we search for food. This is the only cue to which you should respond. If you eat because you are bored or frustrated, you will find it hard to control your weight.

11. *I will occasionally attempt a two- to four-day fast, not only to rest my intestines, but to eliminate some foods to which I may have become sensitive.* If you get a withdrawal headache every time you try a water fast, it usually means that you are allergic to some food you stopped eating, and it would be smart to get away from that food. You are allergic and addicted to it, and it is causing symptoms.

12. *I will try to eat my largest meal for breakfast.* Many weight-control programs are sabotaged because the dieter skips breakfast. The body gets confused messages when there is no fuel available for the day's activities. Overeating may then occur in the evening. Many feel nauseated in the A.M. and cannot eat because they are in acidosis from the binge of carbo eating the previous night. (*See* "Diet If You Have Trouble Getting Out of Bed in the Morning," page 128.) Some studies have shown that when the day's largest meal is eaten in the evening, more of it is converted to body fat than when the same number of calories are eaten earlier in the day.

13. *I will try to eat small, frequent meals.* Four to six small nibblies a day is the best way for most people. Three meals a day got to be the rule when great-grandmother had to fire up the stove because she thought it was important to cook the vegetables. When the body eats infrequently, all the calories cannot be used and storage (as fat) is the net result. It is best not to eat later than two to three hours before retiring, because storage is more likely to take place.

Some Good Ideas about Cooking and Consuming

Cooking foods destroys many vitamins, alters proteins, and neutralizes enzymes found in the foods. These components of foods aid digestion, so fruits and vegetables should be cooked little or not at all.

Many people get muscle cramps and have insomnia if they drink homogenized, pasteurized milk. The assumption is that they cannot absorb the calcium from the milk thus treated. If they drink raw, certified, whole cow's milk, they are free of symptoms, so it cannot be a milk allergy. (One must know the cow, however, and be assured that she was free of diseases.)

Beans and seeds are more nourishing if sprouted.

Meat must be cooked to destroy bacteria and parasite eggs; the cooking breaks down the cell walls in the meat so we can more easily digest and absorb the cellular contents.

Stainless steel, glass, or cast iron are the best (or least poisonous) materials for cooking utensils; some of the metal from aluminum pots may diffuse out into the foods being cooked.

Fried foods are covered with fat and are tough for humans to digest. Olive, safflower, and sunflower oils are probably the better oils to use for cooking. Vitamin E, 400 to 800 units, should be taken by those who eat foods cooked in fat; it protects us from the harmful effects of oxidation in the oils (which are on their way to becoming rancid).

It is probably best to combine certain foods at each meal. Protein and green vegetables are a good combination. Starches combine with vegetables, but do less well with protein. Nuts or seeds can be eaten with citrus fruits. Eat melon by itself; nothing should be combined with it as it is too sweet and impairs the digestion of other foods. Avoid eating sweet fruits (dates, raisins, bananas) together with citrus fruits.

Dentists tell me to spread the word that it is best to drink spring or distilled water and to stay away from soft or fruit drinks. Children who drink the juices instead of eating the fruit itself are not exercising their jaws and are more likely to grow up with a malocclusion.

Vegetarian proteins are nutritionally as good as animal proteins, but some effort must be made to combine the sources to make the protein complete (although Pritikin believes this is not too important). Beans and peas lack the amino acid tryptophan and some of the sulfur-containing amino acids, while nuts, seeds, and grains usually are low in lysine and isoleucine. Adequate lysine seems to be critical for the formation of good protein in the body. Inactivation of the lysine in cereal grains, milk, soy beans, vegetables, and meat occurs when these products are heated for sterilization purposes, as they are in processed foods to prevent spoilage. Young and old are affected by lysine shortage, since it is a major component of collagen. Bones, teeth, blood vessels, and about everything that holds us upright and together has lysine. Therefore, *eat foods as little cooked as possible.*

The following suggestions for vegetable-protein combinations would provide complete proteins or would at least balance the amino acids:

Combine rice with beans, cashews, dairy products, eggs, legumes, spinach, wheat germ, or brewer's yeast.

Beans should be combined with nuts, dairy products, eggs, grains, seeds, rice, or spinach.

Pasta should be eaten with cashews, dairy products, eggs, spinach, or wheat germ.

Peanuts or peanut butter combine well with dairy products, eggs, spinach, and wheat germ.

Most vegetables will provide all the amino acids if eaten with cashews, dairy products, eggs, rice, sunflower seeds, spinach, or wheat germ.

If you make your own bread, you could combine bean flour with the regular grain flour.[1]

The next pages will help you find the ideal, just-right-for-your-physiology, comfortable diet: Take heart! The research findings indicate that fatty acids, amino acids, and calcium release a hormone from the duodenum called CCK (cholecystokinin), which tells the satiety center of the thalamus to tell your body to stop shoveling it in. Eating a little protein with fat at the very beginning of the meal should help one eat a smaller meal. The first part of the meal should be protein anyway, to get the full effect of the stomach acid. Don't eat the salad first—be European. Put your fork down between bites and give your chemistry a chance to work. Think of your ancestors swinging through the trees, eating a mouse here, a banana there. Can you swing if you're fat?

1. An excellent all-round source of nutritional information is Jim Winer's *Basic Nutrition Handbook* (San Diego: Sunshine Press, 8th printing, 1982).

5

Dr. Smith's Low-Stress Weight Control Diet

Whenever anyone does research into the role that diet plays in weight gain, longevity, cancer, heart disease, energy levels, or whatever, they come to more or less the same conclusion: The sick tend to share a history of certain dietary patterns, and so, too, do the healthy ones among us. The government with its dietary goals, the American Heart Association, Nathan Pritikin with his life-saving diet are all saying the same thing: Do choose certain foods and do stay away from others.

Here are the "foods to remember." Tick them off on your fingers:

Fresh fruits

Fresh vegetables

Beans (not canned)

Long grain or brown rice

Whole wheat pasta

Sunflower seeds

Oatmeal, grits, wheat germ, shredded wheat cereals

Whole-grain breads

Baked or poached fish

Nonfat milk, low-fat yogurt, low-fat cheese.

If you continue to eat these foods, you will notice that your blood pressure gets back to normal, your cholesterol falls, your weight levels off around the norm for your height, and you feel good. And most importantly, you will find that your food cravings and addictions will diminish.

The foods to avoid are not so obvious. If you like something and consume it daily, it could be responsible for your low energy and difficulty in losing weight. Anything can do anything. You may be allergic and addicted to sugar, fructose, sucrose, dextrose, maple syrup, chocolate, coffee, molasses, honey. But perhaps you avoid all these and eat only the foods you have been told are good for you. Sorry! Many of the "good" foods—dairy products, soy, beef, corn, wheat, eggs, shellfish, and peanuts—are frequent allergens and have the potential of causing addictions and blood sugar fluctuations that lead to weight gain. Is there a food you love and need to eat every day? If so, it is probably the one that is destroying you, or, at least, disturbing your metabolism to the point that you are gaining instead of losing. If you stop eating this favorite food and experience withdrawal symptoms on the third or fourth day, then you know that you are allergic and addicted to it and that it is important for you to stay off that food.

The Basic Low-Stress Weight Control Diet provides a nice balance of nutritious foods to be eaten in rotation and with all the choices it allows you shouldn't get bored. You should like the Diet after you get used to it, because it is what humans are supposed to eat. Your body will say thank you. The diet works, too. If you eat this way you should feel well enough to want to exercise or at least walk around the block. (That's a start.) If stress is not a factor in your life, you should be able to lose easily on the basic meal plan and then maintain the proper weight for your body. You might even notice that you feel so good that things which used to stress you no longer do so, or do so to a lesser degree.

Once you have branded into your brain the basic philosophy of sound eating, and once you have achieved comfort and are maintaining a reasonable weight for your frame, you should continue with the foods, the sequencing, and the rotation that you know are good for health and longevity. Then you will notice that you can eat some of your old favorites and still be comfortable the next day (those chocolate-dipped strawberries?). I can drink a little milk now, but not every day. I can have a piece of bread occasionally, but if I have a sandwich every day I'll gain 5 pounds in a week. I can even sip some wine without getting a headache. Once you balance your body, you have a margin for indiscretion.

On the Low-Stress Weight Control Diet you think in terms of food groups, not specific food items or specific recipes. You can eat the foods your genes dispose you to be comfortable with, and you can satisfy your whims from day to day. If you feel like having brown rice on Tuesday, fine! No one says you have to have buckwheat groats on Tuesday (or ever).

But the Basic Diet is not the only strategy offered here for weight control. Each one of us has individual needs that have to be met, and there are actual physiological reasons why some people find it harder to lose than others. So I have incorporated the Basic Diet into six different modified approaches that should help just about everyone: those who find losing weight

1. Somewhat Difficult.
2. Moderately Difficult.
3. Fairly Tough.

4. A Real Struggle.

5. Practically Impossible.

6. Impossible without a Stomach-Stapling or Intestinal Bypass operation.

If you find yourself in one of these categories, your feeling of a loss of autonomy due to your inability to lose weight is a stress which, of itself, could be making you *gain* weight. Each of these phases has suggestions for overcoming the particular physiological obstacles to weight control, and especially for lessening the stressful feelings that may be making you fat.

What follows, then, is my Basic Low-Stress Weight Control Diet. My consultant, Dr. Wayne Anderson, a naturopath who has also used it and found it valuable, likes to call it the No-Diet Plan because it really involves a lifestyle change, not just an effort to lose 20 pounds that come back with a vengeance as soon as the diet is abandoned. Study the outline and memorize the principles of eating it sets forth. For help in planning your meals, choose your protein source, starches, vegetables, and fruits from the food list beginning on page 62.

On this basic, generic diet, reasonably normal persons should be able to maintain strength while losing weight, and then be able to hold their weight at the desired level. Ingesting about 1000 to 1300 calories a day should allow for comfort and weight loss. Weight maintenance at the desired level would require a balance between the calories taken in and the calories expended. A moderately active female might manage her weight nicely at about the 2000- to 2500-calorie intake level. The male needs about 2500 to 3000 calories. A vigorously active man would need about 4000 calories. But the active ones should not get the extra food they need from fats and sugars. All the calories (and this goes for everyone) should be contained in wholesome, nourishing foods. To lose weight, and to control it over the long term, make up your meals using the following food groups:

1. *One protein portion per meal.* Lean animal meat is okay, but fish and fowl (without the skin) are better. Try to have legumes, nuts, and grains, and occasionally have meatless days. Lean veal, lamb, pork, and beef have about 130 to 160 calories per 2½- to 3-ounce serving. If you eat about this same amount of sausage or luncheon meat you will be getting over 200 calories: too much fat. A 3-ounce portion of baked fish has about 120 to 140 calories. One boiled egg is 80 calories; frying it adds calories from the fat. One tablespoon of peanut butter will give you 90 calories; most nuts are half fat, so 100 calories are concentrated in just about each tablespoon of the nuts or nut butters. Cottage cheese is but 25 calories to the ounce (2 tablespoons); cream cheese has four times the calories. Try to use yogurt if you use dairy products. Cheese nibblers can shoot their blood triglyceride levels way up because of the fat in the cheese. Most cheeses have about 105 calories per ounce. Skim milk has 90 calories per cup; it has all the good things without the fat. Beans have neither fat nor cholesterol, and ½ cup will have a caloric density of 80 to 110. Whole grains provide bulk, fiber, and the amino acids not always found in the legume. A slice of whole wheat bread contributes about 60 calories, and a bowl of cooked cereal has about 100 calories. Aim to get about 100 to 130 calories from the protein portion of each meal.

2. *One or two vegetable portions per meal.* (See list, "Complex Carbohydrates," p. 63.) Eat the vegetables after the protein has been swallowed. The bulkeffect of vegetables will make you feel full and the appetite center in the hypothalamus will get the message to call a halt to your eating. Low-calorie, high-fiber, leafy vegetables are standard for this suppressing effect. One-half cup of the following vegetables contains but 20 to 40 calories: asparagus, beets, beet greens, broccoli, Brussels sprouts, cooked cabbage, carrots, chard, collards, kale, kohlrabi, cooked onions, spinach, squash, tomatoes, turnips, and turnip

greens. All of these are good sources of the vitamins and minerals you need every day.

Low-calorie vegetables are the dieter's friends. You use more calories chewing up these vegetables than you will get from them once they are digested. They include raw cabbage, cauliflower, celery, cucumbers, lettuce, mushrooms, mustard greens, okra, peppers, and radishes. These have but 5 to 10 calories per 1/2 cup.

Starchy vegetables are what we call complex carbohydrates. You should watch your intake of the starches because they are more calorie-dense; however, it takes the body longer to break down the starches, so they give up their calories over an extended period of time and help to maintain the blood sugar at a more even level than would the same number of calories ingested in simple sugars (as in fruit juices, syrups, and candy). Among the starchy vegetables, cooked corn has 85 calories per 1/2 cup; parsnips, 50 calories; green peas, 60; potatoes have 90 calories in a medium-sized baked potato, while hashed browns have a whopping 230 calories per 1/2 cup; one medium-sized sweet potato will give you 150 calories.

3. *Fruit* should be eaten two to three times a day, but not at the same time as the protein. If they are eaten in the form in which Mother Nature gives them to us, the pectins and fiber in the flesh of the fruit will slow the absorption of the sugar and the body will get a more even and prolonged elevation of the blood sugar. Restrict consumption of fruit juice (drink water instead). A usual serving of fruit (about the size of a medium apple, or about 3 ounces) contains from 35 (in an average-size peach) to 100 calories (in an average-size pear). Dates and raisins contain as much as 250 calories in just a 1/2 cup. Avoid fruit that has been sweetened with table sugar or comes canned in heavy syrup.

If we construct a reasonably balanced, hypoallergenic, nutrient-rich, 1200-calorie diet that would sustain our energy, it will look something like this:

DAILY, BEFORE BREAKFAST

Upon arising and a half-hour before breakfast squeeze half a lemon into a glass of tepid water. Drink it down. This will cleanse and stimulate the stomach. Having liquids upon arising is supposed to help rid the kidneys of some of the overnight wastes that have accumulated. Another drink to promote this is a teaspoonful of chlorophyll in a glass of water.

An exercise physiologist told me years ago "you have to earn your breakfast!" What he meant was that we all should exercise, aerobically, of course, to earn the right to eat something. What he may have discovered is a phenomenon that research has now verified. Those who exercise on an empty stomach are more likely to burn up fat. Those who exercise shortly after a meal seem to burn up only the calories they just ate and will not get rid of the stored lard.

BREAKFAST

One protein portion	150 calories
One cereal or bread portion	100 calories
One starch (complex carbohydrate)	60 calories
One fruit	50 calories

The protein could include a cheese omelette. I will sometimes put some hard cheese (protein) on a piece of whole-wheat bread and melt it in the toaster oven. That and an orange (fruit) would do me nicely and allow me to last until lunch time. How about a piece of toast covered with old-fashioned peanut butter (protein)? And a bowl of applesauce (fruit) after the main course has been digested with the stomach acids? If you use dried fruits, it would be better to soak them in water overnight to leach out some of the sugar.

MIDMORNING SNACK

Vegetables eaten raw; best to use the ones of low calorie
    density
    or
Piece of melon   40–70 calories
    or
Vegetable broth or low-sodium vegetable juice

LUNCH

One starch (complex carbohydrate)   150 calories
Raw vegetables   40–80 calories

Your choice of starch, or complex carbohydrate, could be yellow corn bread, baked potato (yogurt topping), barley, steamed brown rice, wild rice, millet cereal, squash, whole grain bread, oatmeal, RyKrisp, or bran muffins. (Best not to use *too* much unleavened bread, as the zinc will combine with the phytate and will not be absorbed.)

For your vegetables, select from the low-calorie varieties: tomatoes, green leaf lettuce, celery, bean sprouts, green peppers, parsley, watercress, endive, onion, cabbage, spinach, chard, cucumber, zucchini, asparagus. Have them as salad, with low-calorie dressing, or simply washed and trimmed as finger foods. Be creative and colorful.

MIDAFTERNOON SNACK

Fruit and/or nuts   50–100 calories
    or
Vegetable-and-grain soup   100 calories

DINNER

One protein portion	150 calories
Two steamed vegetables	50 calories
One starch	100 calories
Raw salad	50 calories

As your protein, have fish, fowl, lean meats, but avoid fats, pork, and cured meats while trying to lose weight. Legumes and grains are good protein sources.

As your veggies, how about artichokes, beets, carrots, turnips, eggplant, cauliflower, or leeks? See lists on page 64 and in the Appendix (The Page Clinic's Super Seven Food Plan) for more ideas.

The starch would be nicely satisfied by a potato, sweet potato, corn, or peas.

DRINKS

Try to stay away from liquids before or during meals. Drink six to eight glasses of water a day. Try soup broths, coffee substitutes, buttermilk, raw milk, oat straw tea, peppermint tea, papaya tea, alfalfa tea, kefir.

Approximate total calories per day: 1090–1280 calories

We have not laid down specific combinations or menus here, because specifics get tiresome after a while and that's when people tend to fall off their diets. In this new lifestyle you have chosen, *you* will make the decisions about what you eat.

The food lists that follow offer so many combinations of foods that it would be almost impossible to exhaust the possibilities. In addition, if you turn to page 85, you will find eight days of Low-Stress Diet menus. They are designed as extra help for those of you who are troubled with allergies, but they apply equally to anyone who wants to lose weight.

Still more options are to be found in the Appendix's Super Seven Food Plan.

PROTEINS

The following foods are proteins; when digested, they become the amino acids that our bodies need in order to synthesize tissue, hormones, and enzymes. We adults need about 50 to 70 grams of high quality protein per day. Pregnancy, surgery, or stress would raise the demand (up to 90 grams in some cases). Obviously, meat, seafood, dairy products, eggs, and poultry are higher in protein than fruits, but nuts, seeds, grains, beans, and vegetables have a fair amount of protein and less salt and fat than the meats (and no cholesterol).

This list tells how much protein is provided in a 100-gram (3½-ounce) portion. Add up the protein foods you eat in a day until you get the 50 grams or so you need for the twenty-four-hour period. Try to figure 15 grams for breakfast, 15 for lunch, and 15 for supper. If you find that five or six snacks are better for your blood sugar, then get about 10 grams of protein in every time you eat.

GRAMS OF PROTEIN PER 100 GRAMS (3½ ounces) OF FOOD CONSUMED

Food	Protein
Rice, polished	2.0
Yams	2.2
Potatoes, baked in skin	2.6
Broccoli, boiled	3.1
Brussels sprouts, boiled	4.1
Yogurt from skimmed cow's milk	5.9
Lima beans, boiled	8.2
Mixed-grain bread	9.2
Soy beans, boiled	11.0

Eggs, whole	
Cheese, ricotta	
Cheese, cottage, uncreamed	
Lamb chops, medium broiled	18.0
Almonds, raw	19.5
Scallops, steamed	23.2
Flounder, baked	25.0
Chicken, broiled	26.3
Peanuts, raw without skins	26.5
Salmon, baked	27.0
Tuna, canned in water	28.0
Cheese, Swiss, natural	28.8
Beef steak, well done	33.1
Brewer's yeast	38.8
Soy grits	47.3

If you can eat 3 eggs or 3 ounces of soy grits, you will have all the protein you need for one day. You may place any of these protein foods into the menus suggested in the text.

COMPLEX CARBOHYDRATES
(including starches)[1]

Complex carbohydrates are the key to weight control because they provide slowly released energy, as well as fiber, a fair amount of protein, and little or no fat.

In the following group of complex carbohydrates, the calories swallowed would be low in relation to the fiber or roughage. You should feel full, without being overloaded with the calories.

1. This information regarding complex carbohydrates is adapted from *Guidebook to Nutritional Factors in Foods*, by David A. Phillips, Ph.D. (Santa Barbara, Calif.: Woodbridge Press, 1979).

CALORIES PER 100 GRAMS (3½ OUNCES) OF CARBOHYDRATE-CONTAINING FOOD

Food	Calories
Zucchini, boiled*	12
Cucumbers, raw*	14
Squash, summer, boiled*	15
Celery, raw	18
Asparagus, boiled	20
Tomatoes*	22
Spinach, raw	23
Cauliflower, boiled*	24
Broccoli, boiled*	26
Onions, boiled	27
Watermelon	27
Turnips, boiled*	28
Green beans, boiled	30
Carrots, boiled*	30
Beets, boiled*	31
Honeydew melon	34
Brussels sprouts, boiled	38
Apricots	45
Pineapple, raw	52
Apples	57
Grapes	66
Peas, boiled*	70
Figs, fresh, raw	76
Corn, boiled*	83
Bananas	87
Cheese, ricotta	100

The sweeter a food tastes, the quicker the sugar will hit your bloodstream and make your blood sugar rise. The vegetables are more starchy than the fruits, so it takes longer for the

*Denotes starches.

body to break them down; the blood sugar will rise more slowly. These complex carbohydrates provide a more sustained energy. The fruits, however, will give up their sugar more readily because it is stored in the fruits *as sugar*. The fiber and the pectin in the fruits will slow the sugar absorption if the fruit is eaten in its natural state. Fruit sauces and drinks do not contain the fiber needed to delay the sugar absorption.

To achieve a full feeling with fewer calories, choose the foods at the top of the list. As you go down the list the foods become more calorie-dense.

FIBER

Fiber has been proven to be important because it will lower cholesterol, prevent wide swings of blood sugar, and keep the bowel movements soft enough to discourage colon cancer, diverticulitis, hiatal hernia, and hemorrhoids.

GRAMS OF FIBER PER CUP (8 OUNCES) OF FOOD CONSUMED

Food	Fiber
Millet, whole grain, dry	7.3
Blackberries, raw	5.9
Sunflower seeds	5.5
Figs, dried	5.6
Raw wheat bran	5.2
Avocado	4.2
Peanuts, almonds, raw	4.0
Peas, cooked	3.2
Rye flour, dark, soft	3.0
Lima beans, cooked	3.0
Rice bran	2.4
Lettuce	0.3
Dried prunes	1.6

Many sufferers from constipation and associated sluggishness need only add 1 to 4 teaspoons of miller's bran to soup or cereal each day to get the proper texture to their bowel movements. If that does not budge the reluctant stools, then one should look to the state of the thyroid gland. Hypothyroidism usually makes the victim constipated.

PHASE ONE: SOMEWHAT DIFFICULT TO LOSE

Probably the best way to begin if you find it "somewhat difficult" to lose is to see a doctor for a baseline physical and laboratory exam. Some chiropractors and naturopaths are more helpful with this than orthodox M.D.s, who would just as soon treat a *bona fide* illness. Find out your height and weight and compare your vital statistics with the Metropolitan Life Insurance tables for longevity as a function of size. (Notice that weights listed on these tables include an allowance of several pounds for clothing.) Have your doctor take your pulse and blood pressure. It would be smart to have an electrocardiogram and a chest X ray taken for baseline heart function and size. Make sure blood is drawn for a complete blood count, cholesterol, glucose level, high- and low-density lipoproteins, and triglycerides, and get some liver function tests. Include the thyroid tests (T3 and T4);* you might suggest that some blood be saved for a thyroid-stimulating hormone test in case the T3 and T4 are abnormal. You might also ask for a stress test to see how your heart does with exercise. The doctor should ask about your diet, your allergies, from where you get your calcium, vitamin C, selenium, and vitamin E. How are your bowel movements? Fiber? How much sugar each day? Cigarettes? Coffee? Alcohol? Exercise? Stresses should be evaluated. Tell the doctor about diseases in the family. Were you a fat child? Who died at what age of what disease? You must report symptoms. What drugs do you take daily? Does your doctor ask you if you are comfortable?

*T3 and T4 are the circulating levels of the active thyroid hormone floating about in the bloodstream.

If all these tests and questions are normal or nonrevealing, and you have a minimal stress but need to lose weight, start right in with the Basic Dr. Smith's Low-Stress Weight Control Diet. In choosing your foods, the low-fat vegetarian foods will probably give you the best results. However, if your thyroid, cholesterol, and triglycerides are okay, you could compromise and have a piece of beef and some low-fat milk (2 percent) and some nuts and seeds weekly. But you have to know the risks and you must monitor your symptoms. If you eat animal protein and fats and sugars, you may set yourself up for cardiovascular disease; you may stress your thyroid. *Any* symptom—headache, fatigue, gas, constipation, frequent infections, skin rashes, high blood presure, shortness of breath, insomnia, muscle aches, irritability, whatever—might mean that your body is objecting to your lifestyle and your diet. Many of my recommendations regarding food sequencing and dieting are fairly new ideas which have arisen out of my frequent discussions with fellow nutritionists and clinicians across the country. This recommended eating style seems so logical and natural that I wish I had thought about it years ago. (A particularly good plan used by the Page Clinic in Saint Petersburg Beach, Florida, for real problem dieters is featured in the Appendix.

The important points to learn are that most foods are okay for the body if (1) they are eaten in small amounts, and (2) they are ingested in the proper sequence. On this diet you eat the protein first, then legumes and grains, followed by the vegetables in this order: root, white, green, colored, and leafy (salad).

Protein needs acid for its digestion; by ingesting water, fruit, or salad before the protein, you dilute the hydrochloric acid, and the protein cannot receive its full digestive allotment of acid. Result: putrefaction. The Page Clinic stops dairy products for the first month and does not allow the participants to eat fruit anywhere near the protein portion of the meal. Sometimes this sequencing is the only change dieters make in their eating habits, and they begin to have more energy and less gas.

The tissues of our bodies cannot get along just with protein, fats, and carbohydrates; they also must have the full allotment of minerals and vitamins. For weight loss to occur, the sluggish machinery of the overweight body must burn the stored fat to carbon dioxide and water. This process requires some special supplements, because all those good vegetables, grains, and legumes we are eating don't necessarily have all the vitamins and minerals in them that we buy them for. If the minerals are not in the topsoil where the plants grow, you and I are not going to get them. An all-purpose vitamin and mineral supplement would be a prudent addition just in case one feels cheated. Getting the Recommended Daily Allowances (RDAs) is what you are after right now. The RDAs are the minimum the body needs to be able to do something. To achieve optimum performance, however, the body will need more of at least some of the vitamins and minerals. If you have symptoms (as above), or if you are overweight, then it suggests that your body is already deficient in some or all of these nutrients.

Taking digestive enzymes with each meal would be one way to help the intestines break down the foods into their component, absorbable parts: amino acids, fatty acids, and simple sugars. These enzyme preparations usually contain hydrochloric acid, bile acid, pancreatic enzymes, and papaya.

While the body is burning its fat stores, some attention must be paid to the liver. This organ has at least five hundred functions, one of which is to act as a filter. As the blood circulates through the liver, the liver cells grab fats from the blood and manufacture bile salts and hormones out of the fats. A lot of fat (a steak for dinner, with butter on the potato, and an eclair for dessert) can overload the capacity of the liver to store and metabolize these fats. During weight reduction, fats are mobilized from the stores around the body and are used as energy.

A clean liver is needed to do all this work, and we can aid it in doing its job efficiently. First, you must eat no spices, pepper, mustard, or take any tobacco, alcohol, or drugs during weight loss, because these things irritate the liver. Supplements can make you comfortable in getting off your addictions. Certain nutrients called lipotropics help clear the liver of fatty deposits; choline and inositol, 500 mg of each, should be taken twice daily. Methionine, 1000 mg a day, is valuable in aiding the liver. This and other sulfur-containing amino acids (cystine, cysteine, taurine) are found in garlic, onions, red peppers, chives, and eggs. Garlic is helpful in lowering triglycerides and cholesterol in the blood and seems to lower the blood sugar level.

B_6, 100 mg, is to be taken once a day and then increased daily until dream recall is good. B_6 is important as a coenzyme for a number of liver enzyme functions. Excessive pyridoxine, above 1000 to 2000 mg a day, can lead to a sensory neuropathy with numbness and tingling of the fingers and toes. The use of lecithin to help clear fats from the body is standard, but the capsules become rancid and worthless rapidly. Use the granules; best to look for phosphatidyl choline. These factors would be used daily for a month and then for one-month periods two or three times a year depending upon fat accumulation and the levels in the bloodstream.

Naturopaths often recommend a beet-juice fast for three days to clean the liver. (If the urine turns red, it suggests the ingester is anemic.) Another juice fast consists of squeezing ten lemons into 2 quarts of water, adding a touch of honey, and drinking a glassful every two hours. If you are up to it, you should continue this for four days (!). It rests the liver and can help get you off the foods to which you are addicted. Here is another liver-cleansing routine: In the A.M. on arising you may drink as much carrot or beet juice as you like; at noon eat vegetable soup with brown rice plus a steamed potato and a green salad. In the evening a salad, vegetable, and brown rice. Between meals you may eat raw apples. Herbal teas would be okay. The idea of this is to rest the liver and let it catch up, since there are no fats, no protein, and no fried foods in this one-day cleansing menu. Excessive circulating fats are hard on the body and the liver can get sludged up from them.

Everything takes about a month, and it will be successful if you are comfortable with it. You might have lost 4 to 8 pounds in the last thirty days and felt good while you were doing it. You should notice that most of the symptoms described on page 67 have subsided. If it works, stick with it. If it does not work, go on to Dr. Smith's Low-Stress Diet, Phase Two.

PHASE TWO: MODERATELY DIFFICULT TO LOSE

Try the six-meals-a-day routine, with each meal being of equal caloric and protein equivalents. If you are about to eat a 4-ounce piece of meat, cut it in half; eat half now, and stick the other 2 ounces in your doggy bag or pocket or purse to eat in about two to three hours. You should notice that you are less hungry and eat less when the regular meals come around.

Now add a B-complex capsule that has close to the following amounts. Take it three times a day with some food.

B_1, 50 mg

B_2, 50 mg

B_3, 50 mg; this usually comes as niacinamide (it would be good if you could take 50 mg of niacin also)

B_6, 50 mg; you are already taking this, but it is usually part of the B-complex formulation

B_{12}, 100 mcg

Folic acid, 0.4 mg

Inositol, 250 mg*

*You can discontinue the amounts suggested for Phase One dieters.

Choline, 500 mg*

PABA, 50 mg

Biotin, 100 mcg

This formula should provide energy and even cheerfulness. It also helps in digesting food, as the B vitamins are involved in all the enzyme systems of the body. You should notice that your urine is a rich yellow color; it does not mean a waste of vitamins. It means you are absorbing the riboflavin, B_2, at least, and the excess is being excreted. (Some of the vitamins on the market are worthless; they have so many fillers and stabilizers that the pills go right through you. In general it is better to get the vitamins from a professional source.)

In about two to three weeks' time on the vitamins you should notice that your energy level is up enough so that you can stay up later at night and even walk to the store and around the block. Some notice a temporary increase in appetite; that will quiet down soon. If you think the B-complex vitamins are making you sick, it suggests you have a yeast infection. If the vitamins have a stimulating effect, or if your dreams are so vivid that you are wakeful, it suggests that you are low in calcium. The B vitamins release histamine from the basophil cells of the body. Calcium, about 1000 mg, along with the same amount of magnesium, should solve the problem.

(*Note:* We used to recommend that calcium be taken at about the 1000-mg level and magnesium at about half that, or 500 mg. Now we have discovered that magnesium deficiency is widespread in the population, and the recommended prudent dose for all has been revised by some authorities to 1000 mg, equal to the calcium. Usually it was suggested that the two minerals be taken at bedtime, since they have a calming effect. Some recent evidence seems to indicate that they could compete for entrance into the body, however, and thus should be taken at separate times, about an hour apart.)

Nothing is more difficult than getting the heavy lethargic

ones to exercise. I have found that if I can get them to eat better and take some supplements, they begin to feel more like moving after about one to three weeks. Walking as briskly as possible about 100 to 200 yards is a start and is best done before breakfast. At this time, after a twelve-hour fast, the body is more likely to burn up the stored fat. This little amount of exercise plus the B-complex vitamins should help activate the enzymes in the mitochondria.

If you are hypoglycemic or a mature-onset diabetic, you will be helped with the glucose tolerance factor (GTF), which consists mainly of vitamin B_3 and chromium. This GTF is found abundantly in brewer's yeast because the yeast is grown in chrome-steel vats and the chromium leaches out into the plant. Some diabetics have found they were able to reduce their insulin dose in just ten to fourteen days. The insulin becomes more efficient as more receptor sites are opened up. Most mature-onset diabetics are overweight; the diets in this book would help them lose the weight *and* the diagnosis. People with the yeast problem (candidiasis) find that yeasty things really make them sick. The yeast in their intestines feeds on the yeast they are ingesting (wine, beer, cheese, bread, yeast; also, most B vitamins are made from yeast, so it would be better for these people to get their B vitamins from bacterial synthesis[2] or from rice polishings, and to get their chromium from a reliable professional source).

After about two to three weeks of this B-complex and minimal exercise intervention, about 40 percent of those who try this approach will find their answer, and nothing more need be done except to increase the exercise to the tolerance level and cut out all the sugar. Eliminating beef products and restricting dairy food intake to one day out of every four or five days would

2. Available from the Allergy Research Group, 2336-C Stanwell Circle, Concord, CA 94520.

help. Remember, most cheese is 50 to 75 percent fat. The not-so-successful ones might now move on to Phase Three.

PHASE THREE: FAIRLY TOUGH TO LOSE

The B-complex vitamins are essential for the work of the enzyme systems that are involved with digestion, absorption, and metabolism. But many people are not able to absorb the B complex in sufficient quantities to allow all this to happen. The absorptive mechanism in the intestines must be working well enough to absorb the vitamins and minerals necessary to promote the absorption of the vitamins and minerals necessary to help the enzymes absorb. You have to be healthy to be healthy.

Years ago I began to give vitamin B-complex shots to the hyperactive and allergic children in my practice. Typically, the mothers would come in saying these children were gaining weight and eating half as much food. Malabsorption! It seemed so logical. These hyper children cannot get enough of the nutrients the body needs, so they eat huge amounts of the foods set before them. When we got them on a good diet and stopped the dairy products, the intestinal enzymes must have improved to the extent that they could efficiently digest and absorb the foods. The vitamin shots were an adjunct to all this.

So I began to give these shots to adults who were pale, exhausted, sick, apathetic, depressed, gaseous, surly, insomniacal or somnolent—whatever. My extensive use of these rather cheap but painful shots indicated to me that many of us cannot get well because we are sick.

The sickness seems to be a function of the competence of the cells that line the intestinal tract. These cells produce enzymes which, along with the stomach acid and pepsin, bile, and pancreatic juices, split the fats, carbohydrates, and proteins down to their simple fatty acids, simple sugars, and amino acids. If these enzymes cannot function, we are unable to digest the foods we swallow. So the health of these lining cells is essential. Stress can interfere with their function. If we continue to eat a diet that is high in calorie-dense, vitamin- and mineral-poor foods, these enzymes cannot operate optimally to split the foods for absorption. The foods will sit in the gut, decompose, and lose much of their value for our bodies. Fats become rancid, carbohydrates ferment, and protein putrefies. When proteins are not digested properly, the bacteria in the intestines go to work on them and turn some of them into cadaverine and putrescene. Imagine what those do to your breath!

The body will use any available minerals and B-complex vitamins floating about in the circulation to activate these intestinal enzymes for this essential digestion-absorption function. This tends to deplete other enzymes in the body and to impair other organ systems.

If foods are not broken down into their simple components in the intestines, they may be absorbed as "foreign" substances and act as allergens. Food allergies may cause hypoglycemia; hypoglycemia may cause weight gain or other symptoms.

B-complex injections help the sufferer break out of this Catch-22. I use the product of the Darby/Rugby Laboratory of New York (B complex no. 7).[3] Merit Laboratory has one called B-plex no. 100 which is quite good for getting the body going.[4] About 0.5 to 0.8 ml is injected intramuscularly two times a week for three weeks. Some are improved with 5 mg of zinc sulfate, i.m., and manganese, 2 mg, i.m. The energy level should be up and the weight down by 2 to 5 pounds in this space of time; one would be able to tell that it is working. It is cheap and safe. Many give their own shots in the thigh, buttocks, or shoulder muscle. Most scream a little because the stuff stings, but about

3. Each ml contains thiamine, 50 mg; riboflavin, 5 mg; niacinamide, 75 mg; pyridoxine, 5 mg; panthenol, 6 mg; cyanocobalamin, 100 mcg; ascorbic acid, 50 mg.
4. Each ml contains thiamine, 100 mg; riboflavin, 2 mg; niacinamide, 125 mg; pyridoxine, 2 mg; and panthenol, 10 mg.

1000 mg of calcium orally about an hour or two before the shot will dull the pain of the muscle spasm and preclude the chance of a reaction from the histamine release. Some add a drop or two of 2 percent procaine into the syringe with the vitamins just prior to injecting; it deadens the pain in just a minute or two.

I have had a number of patients who report to me that they did not change their diet in any significant way but were conscientious about the shots and they lost weight. About 20 to 30 percent of the reluctant losers find weight reduction simplified with these injections. (Does the pain make some lose weight?) The B complex is necessary for energy expenditure in the body, and when given this way it must go right to the depleted enzymes in the intestinal lining cells, improving their efficiency. I would also suspect that the lower-brain enzymes which are supposed to respond to an adequate blood sugar level are now able to send the proper messages to the upper brain: "Stop eating!" The neocortex—where we live—is able to tell the body, "I can do it." Motivation is easier. From the remotest cell to the higher centers of organization in the central nervous system, function is more efficient.

Most Phase Three responders tell me, "I have more energy, and yet I'm calmer." The world seems less close and threatening. Stress is not perceived so acutely.

My view of these people is that they are in a nutritional hole due to stress, injuries, infections, childbirth (mother or child), and an inappropriate diet. Their overweight condition is as much a degenerative disease as is migraine, asthma, arthritis, colitis, or high blood pressure. Stress, bad diets, and genetic factors combine to deplete their enzyme systems. One man's eczema is another's obesity. And the stress of being obese is enough to deplete the body so that the obesity is perpetuated. The same principles of treatment apply to most of these illnesses.

If I can push them out of this nutritional rut with a good diet, encouragement, and the B-complex injections, then the enzymatic pumps are primed (throw kerosene on the embers, crank the engine, start the flywheel). Once the machinery is working efficiently and the intestinal enzymes are absorbing the nutrients they need, the body should be able to continue at its optimal metabolic rate with more normal physiological quantities of supplements. It is just possible that three meals a day may not be enough for most of us to get all the vitamins and minerals we need. Some need these B-complex shots only once a week or once a month to satisfy the hunger enzymes. Some need them more often. (Former prisoners of war are never able to maintain optimum health using only a good diet and the RDA supplements.)

The supplemented (orally or intramuscularly) folk should feel so much better about their easy weight loss—2 to 4 pounds a week without trying too hard—and the return of some of the lost feelings of energy, that they are able to exercise more and even enjoy it. Most regular exercisers get a high from running, playing ball, tennis, skiing, swimming, or just walking.

Exercisers know that they cannot just run off the fat, however. One pound of fat represents about 4000 calories of stored energy. A mile run in about eight minutes will use about 100 calories, so forty miles will be required to combust a pound. A slow loss of no more than 1 or 2 pounds per week is about the ideal goal. A hundred pounds in a year would be great for someone who needs to lose that much. It is attainable.

The next phase of the weight management program is for those not able to respond to the six meals, the B complex, and the mild exercise program.

PHASE FOUR: A REAL STRUGGLE TO LOSE

Most of us who are trying to help people with a nutritional and preventive approach to weight control know how common are food allergies, or more accurately, food sensitivities. Most victims of this debilitating and boring problem are addicted to the very food that is causing the symptoms of the weight gain. Sugar and chocolate are the two most craved foods, but since anything can do anything, the list is a copy of the foods considered superior and essential: milk and dairy products, soy beans, corn, eggs, wheat, nuts, tomato, shellfish, citrus, and all the rest.

One must pause for a moment and reflect on what food is eaten daily. If you love milk and drink it daily, you are probably allergic and addicted to it. It is well known that the ingestion of allergens will make the blood sugar rise and fall.[5] The food sensitivity section of the American College of Allergists has stated that 80 percent of those with food sensitivities have low blood sugar, or hypoglycemia. Without this energy source available for use, calories are stored as fat. Failure to lose weight on a good nibbling diet usually is due to this one phenomenon—the addictive-allergic syndrome. We have many patients who simply cannot lose weight until they stop that particular food they are eating daily.

Milk, wheat, eggs, corn, and beef seem to be the most likely offenders that one must discontinue during this phase. Oriental people develop sensitivities to rice, soy, and fish, and must leave these alone for a week or two. With Latin Americans, the usual villain is corn.

If food allergy is a partial answer, one should know in just a few days of abstinence, or partial fast. I don't have milk more than once a month on some cereal. Cheese and beef are occasional foods for me; I just don't need any headaches, bloat, or nose bleeds. But I did not realize how insidious is my sensitivity to wheat—and I love bread, toast, cookies, even wheat germ. If I avoid all wheat-bearing foods for a week, I can lose 3 pounds of embarrassing lard around my middle. (Running around the block a few times must be done simultaneously.) As a confir-

5. William H. Philpott, M.D., and Dwight K. Kalita, Ph.D., *Brain Allergies: The Psycho-nutrient Connection* (New Canaan, Conn.: Keats Publishing Co., 1980).

mation of this addiction, I now am able to recall eating the inside of a loaf of bread on my way home from the store at age eight years. We had holey toast for a week.

This phase, dealing with allergies and addictions, follows other suggestions for weight control because it is virtually *impossible* to stp an addiction without some vitamin and mineral supports. When the blood sugar falls and the craving for the food hits, the strong become weak, the determined forget their pledges. The neocortex just sits there, unnourished, while the animal, selfish hypothalamus takes over.

Some ask, "Does the craving indicate a basic need for that food?" It is hard to believe that someone could have a chocolate deficiency or a potato chip need. But there is a logic in the process that helps to explain the chemistry of a craving. First, the ingested allergen forces the blood sugar to rise. Insulin is secreted during this rise, and subsequently the blood sugar falls. This drop triggers a search for the favorite food. The biochemically trapped victim has learned which food makes him feel better faster. He eats it and is comfortable in fifteen to thirty minutes. He is addicted. As noted before, when the blood sugar falls, the neocortex, with its built-in ability to organize self-control or to remember previous promises, does not have enough energy flowing through it to do its jobs.

We know that drug addictions can be alleviated and even controlled by large daily doses of vitamin C;[6] 50 to 60 grams (50,000 to 60,000 mg) orally per day allow the addict to manufacture his own endorphins without which the withdrawal symptoms would be too overwhelming to ignore. Vitamin C does seem to help some people get off the foods they love and which they suspect are sabotaging their diet plans.

Dr. William Philpott has found that the carbohydrate dysmetabolism that follows the ingestion of sensitizing foods can be abolished temporarily with the following:

6. Irwin Stone, *The Healing Factor, Vitamin C Against Disease* (New York: Grosset & Dunlap, 1972).

Vitamin C, 1000 mg; calcium (or sodium) ascorbate may
be better than plain ascorbic acid

Calcium, 1000 mg

Vitamin B_6, 200–300 mg

These, if given an hour before a food challenge, a birthday
party, a DPT (diphtheria-pertussis-tetanus immunization vac-
cine) shot, a blast of irritating petrochemicals (like a walk near
traffic) or the ingestion of food dyes, will effectively prevent the
high rapid rise of the blood sugar and the subsequent precipitous
fall with its attendant miseries.

There is no doubt that nibbling on nonallergenic complex
carbohydrates and ingesting the above group of supplements
will keep the blood sugar from fluctuating and triggering the
foraging behavior.

Some Phase Four types will undergo food allergy tests. The
tests are not completely accurate and may lead people to embark
on a long-term food avoidance that may not be necessary or even
prudent. Skin tests for food allergies are considered by most
authorities to be about 20 percent accurate. Allergy testing by
the infradermal provocative method of Joseph Miller, M.D.,
Mobile, Alabama, is accurate for food testing. Miller's method
provides neutralizing doses which are safe for the patient to self-
administer twice weekly for neutralization of the allergic state.
The RAST, which requires a blood sample, is about 60 to 80
percent reliable, depending upon the laboratory. The cytotoxic
test is also in that range. Sublingual testing for sensitivities has
a high correlation but seems to vary with the skill and enthusiasm
of the users.

The four-day fast, with the participant drinking only distilled
water or spring water (or some type of pure water from the
health food store that is free of chlorine, petrochemicals, fluoride, etc.), is the most accurate way to determine food sensitivities. Many, however, are reluctant even to try it. If a patient
says to me, "I couldn't do that! I need to eat every two to three

hours or I faint from weakness," then I know the patient is hooked on some food that is causing the blood sugar swings. But if they can stick out the fast with the encouragement of a supportive family, friends, the doctor, and the B complex, C, and calcium, the rewards are worth it.

The pancreas will secrete less insulin if no food is coming into the body to make the blood sugar rise. The blood sugar will sink slowly over the four or five days. Hunger is less of a problem than the faster thought it would be. The third day may be full of withdrawal symptoms (irritability, restlessness, fatigue, headache, depression), but the fourth day will be like a sprouting of a new way of feeling. It takes this long to get the toxic products formed as a result of the food allergies out of the body. If the withdrawal symptoms are devastating, it is surely an encouraging sign to the faster that he or she is on the right track.

Many fasters have told me how helpful enemas were during these withdrawal periods. The relief they obtained must be due to the fact that they were able to eliminate yeast or to expel allergens or the toxic products that resulted from incompletely digested foods. But too many or too frequent enemata could be dangerous because of the chance of introducing infection, making the patient waterlogged, or washing out some important nutrients.

The "cleansed" faster now starts to eat a new food each day until the previously bothersome symptoms return: food craving, headaches, nervousness, surliness, whatever. The foods that are causing the symptoms are left out of the diet for months or forever. Most people can tolerate their known allergenic foods if they eat them but once every four days. However, if the frequency of ingestion increases, the allergy could recur. Milk allergy causes the body to produce a number of chemicals other than histamine. It may take at least three weeks of abstinence from the dairy foods before slow-reacting substances and some other irritants disappear. With other foods it takes but four to five days. Some find that their allergies are fixed; the food can never safely be ingested again. This is most commonly true of milk. Sensitivity to milk may manifest itself in the infant as ear infections and later, in the forty-year-old, as obesity. Occasionally a ninety-day fast from a particular food will allow that sensitizing food to be reintroduced on an infrequent basis.

But an allergic tendency never vanishes. Many find the avoidance/fasting/rotation diet helpful in itself, but the improvement of body function and the minimizing of the allergies is greatly facilitated by the use of supplements that are specific to enhance the function of the adrenal glands.

Allergies are a stress and the adrenals are the first to complain. If you think it possible that food allergies may explain your inability to lose weight, then the following supplements may speed your recovery to normal metabolism and weight control.

Vitamin C seems to be the key to allergy control, whether the symptoms are due to inhalants or to food. Inhalant allergies mean the adrenal glands are not functioning properly. This is a stress and could contribute to poor weight management. If inhalant allergies are present, food sensitivities often are present although more difficult to diagnose. Most inhalants are mediated by immunoglobulin E (IgE, a protein in the blood), and usually are diagnosed by skin tests. Food sensitivities create their reactions by different biochemical mechanisms.

Vitamin C can improve both allergies and sensitivities. People find their own dose by increasing the vitamin C (calcium or sodium ascorbate may be better than plain vitamin C) by 1000 mg each day; for example, 1000 mg on Monday, 2000 mg on Tuesday, 3000 mg on Wednesday. This is continued until one's bowel movements are softened slightly. This is the saturation dose and it is continued as the daily dose for long-term control of the allergy. It is increased if one perceives that one is in the middle of a stressful situation. Or it is increased for infections; the daily dose is taken every hour with the result that the duration and severity of the disease should be lessened. It might also be increased if someone forces you to eat some candy or drink some alcohol.

Pantothenic acid, 200 to 1000 mg a day, is a well-known, safe, allergy-control B vitamin. It helps get C into the cells. It is a cortisol precursor; large doses provide the raw material to aid the body in the manufacture of cortisol. With adequate cortisol, the allergy should be calmed in a natural way.

B_6, 100 to 300 mg a day, in addition to the B complex, seems to help the body control allergies.

Calcium, 1000 mg, usually taken at bedtime, is a histamine antagonist, so it is valuable in allergic conditions. Most take 1000 mg of *magnesium* as well. These two minerals have a calming effect. It might be best to take the calcium and magnesium an hour apart. No big deal; it is just that some authorities believe they are absorbed better if they are not taken together.

Some in this category have discovered that all they needed to do was take a digestive enzyme tablet with each meal. Most of these formulations have hydrochloric acid, pancreatic enzymes, bile acid, papaya, and other ingredients to imitate the stomach and intestinal digestive juices. The carbohydrates are more completely broken down into simple sugars, the fats become fatty acids, and the proteins become the small component amino acids. These simple, easy-to-absorb foods are nonallergenic and don't cause the blood sugar to bounce up and down, leading to weight gain.

Some discouraged dieters with food allergies have found that raw adrenal and thymus tissue packaged as a palatable pill has helped them get over allergies.

Most doctors concerned with allergies have discovered that the four-day rotation diet is mandatory for the dedicated dieter. Here, then, are some examples of a varied, rotating diet: it is a meal plan that should help you skirt around your allergies.[7] Do

7. For another approach, see Natalie Golos and Frances Golos Golbitz's *If This Is Tuesday, It Must Be Chicken!* (New Canaan, Conn.: Keats Publishing Co., 1983).

not eat the same food or a food from a group more frequently than every four days. (If you have it on Monday, don't eat it or a like food until Friday.)

The best way to identify a food allergy is to use the four-day water fast. But many are frightened by the thought of going without *some* food for FOUR days. The elimination diet is less drastic; it cuts out the foods you normally eat more than two or three times a week. Instead, you eat foods that are relatively safe (with low allergy potential), but are rarely part of your diet. The following are usually safe, but must be rotated also.[8]

Protein: Turkey, salmon, lamb, duck, rabbit, wild game.

Vegetables: Sweet potato, broccoli, cauliflower, turnip, beet, asparagus, squash.

Fruits: Plum (fresh), prune, pear, nectarine.

Cereals: Rice, oats, rye, and barley.

The goal is to put together low-calorie meals, amounting to about 1000 to 1200 calories a day, using ingredients that are not too strange or too different from what you are used to. These menus show the way. If they help you to be comfortable while attaining your ideal weight, it suggests that you might do well to use these and similar menus for the rest of your life.

DAY 1	DAY 2	DAY 3	DAY 4
Protein:			
beef, lamb, crab, shrimp, cod, haddock, dairy products	turkey, tuna, whitefish	pork, clam, scallop, squid, octopus, salmon, bass, trout, rabbit	chicken, duck, egg, halibut, sole

8. William G. Crook, M.D., *Tracking Down Hidden Food Allergy* (Jackson, Tenn.: Professional Books, 1981).

Vegetables:

corn, tomato, potatoes, eggplant, mushroom	beet, chard, spinach, olive, cucumber, squash, zuc- chini	carrot, celery, parsley, let- tuce, arti- choke, sweet potato, endive	asparagus, garlic, onions, broccoli, cab- bage, Brussels sprouts, pea- nuts, soybeans, beans, peas, cauliflower

Fruits:

currant, grape, raisin	banana, apricot, cherry, peach, nec- tarine, prune, plum, blueberry, cranberry, melon, watermelon	strawberry, raspberry, blackberry, pineapple	grapefruit, fig, lemons, limes, oranges, pa- paya

What follows now are menus for eight days of the rotation diet to show that it can all be very interesting. The diet is hypoallergenic and low-calorie. It seems in line with Pritikin's ideas about the use of whole grains and lots of vegetables. It is also in line with "Atkins" because there is animal protein, al- though the emphasis is on fish and fowl. These menus are fairly high in fiber also. Oat bran might be better than wheat bran, and everyone should become familiar with and use buckwheat kasha, or groats. It is high in potassium and has more vitamin B than wheat. It is an excellent source of protein, and the calories are equivalent to other grains. It is sometimes hard to find so look on the specialty shelves in your grocery store or market, and it takes a certain amount of ingenuity to make it pleasant tasting: mixing it with eggs and onion is one way. You may also want to refer to Sally Rockwell's very helpful rotation material, providing charts, folders, and management ideas.[9]

9. *The Rotation Game* (pamphlet, workbook, and chart), P.O. Box 15181, Seattle, WA 98115.

I feel that the rotation-diet concept has value for most of us. It might solve the problems of truck drivers, lactating mothers, senior citizens, and surly children. The following menus show the calorie counts in the various meals; most dieters find that they can count calories in their heads after a time.

BREAKFAST

1 cup cooked oatmeal, regular	130
½ cup yogurt (low-fat)	80
¼ cup raisins	116
	326 calories

LUNCH

1 cup cottage cheese (low-fat)	200
1 cup diced pineapple, raw (or canned in own juice)	80
2 RyKrisp crackers	50
	330 calories

DINNER

3- ounce beef patty, 3 inches across by ⅝ inch thick (only 10 percent fat)	185
½ cup corn or 1 small ear	70
Salad:	
2 tomatoes	66
½ green pepper	7
1 cup mushrooms	20
Dressing:	
1 teaspoon corn oil	42
1 teaspoon wine vinegar	2
pinch of oregano	—
	392 calories

These three meals give a total caloric count of 1048 calories. But if you were aware as you read over the menu, you may have noticed that beef, milk, and corn are featured, common allergens. If you use these products one day, don't repeat them for four or five days. These menus also give you an idea about how foods differ in their ratios of protein size to calorie content. For example, a snack of two Brazil nuts would give you 57 calories, and 1 cup of popcorn (plain with no butter) would give you 40 calories. It is hard to find filling snacks that are tasty *and* low-calorie unless you use raw vegetables. If you need bran, remember that 1 tablespoon of oat bran has 22 calories; ⅓ cup provides 110 calories. The foods in the foregoing day's menu are nutrient-dense and should give you about everything you need. It would be prudent to continue with the vitamin and mineral supplements (*see* page 70).

All right, then, how about this one? It should carry you through the day on only 1107 calories, and it has few of the common allergens.

BREAKFAST

15 (15, that's it) almonds	169
1 banana	87
¾ cup cherries	63
	319 calories

LUNCH

½ cup mackerel, canned in water with bones	137
1 cucumber	31
3 olives, large Mission type	45
2 plums	78
	291 calories

DINNER

3 ounces turkey	216
1 yam, baked with skin	155
Salad:	
½ pound spinach	59
½ cup beets, boiled	27
Dressing:	
1 teaspoon olive oil, pinch ginger	40
	497 calories

Here is another whole-day menu composed of foods with minimal allergy potential:

BREAKFAST

1 raw apple with peel, *or*	
1 cup of unsweetened apple sauce	100
5 dates	107
10 filberts (2 stuffed into each date)	93
	300 calories

LUNCH

4 ounces scallops, steamed	127
Salad:	
½ head lettuce	30
½ medium carrot, shredded	11
6 tablespoons parsley	4
6 artichoke hearts, cooked	44
Dressing:	
½ tablespoon sunflower oil, cider vinegar	60
1 pear	100
	376 calories

DINNER

4 ounces sea bass, broiled or baked	120
½ cup kasha (buckwheat groats), cooked	100
Parsleyed steamed vegetables:	
1 cup carrots, sliced	21
½ cup parsnips, sliced	51
1 tablespoon parsley, chopped	5
1 cup blackberries	84
	381 calories

This last one will give a total of 1057 calories. If you are aiming for 1100 calories total all day, then you may have a few snacks; 2 stalks of celery is 14 calories; 1 cup of strawberries is 50.

The following menus, for Day Four through Day Seven, will give you ideas for variety so that the foods are rotated; they provide plenty of protein and fiber. If they are nutritionally lacking in any way, it would be in calcium, since dairy products are not emphasized; I would suggest that 1000 mg of calcium and about the same amount of magnesium be taken on a daily basis. Remember, you can juggle these around and use lunch or supper for breakfast just for fun.

BREAKFAST

2- egg omelet	160
1 stalk green onions or chives	8
1 orange	100
	268 calories

LUNCH

Soup made from:

1 cup lentils, cooked	192
1 leek stalk	18
½ onion	20
1 garlic clove	3
½ to 1 teaspoon soy or tamari sauce	7
2 dried figs	114
(Water to cover; simmer until palatable)	
	354 calories

DINNER

3 ounces roast chicken (½ breast or a leg and thigh without skin)	156
Stir-fry vegetables:	
1 onion	40
1 cup cabbage	24
1 cup mung bean sprouts	32
1 tablespoon sesame seeds	81
1 tsp. soy or tamari sauce	7
1 cup papaya, cubed	71
	411 calories

These three meals add up to 1033 calories. You could then splurge and have these snacks in between the meals: half a grapefruit is 58 calories. A tangerine is 39 calories. Nibble, nibble.

Here begins the fifth day. This breakfast takes only a couple of minutes to fix:

BREAKFAST

1 pita bread round (whole-wheat)	125
1 ounce slice low-fat cheese (e.g., part-skim mozzarella)	96
¾ cup pineapple juice	104
	325 calories

LUNCH

1 cup whole-wheat spaghetti, cooked	100
Sauce:	
½ cup tomato sauce	40
½ cup mushrooms	10
1 tbsp. Parmesan cheese	27
1 small bunch grapes	100
	277 calories

DINNER

Shrimp Creole:	
4½ ounces shrimp (or fish of choice, if you are allergic)	100
1 cup brown rice, cooked	200
½ cup tomato sauce	40
½ green pepper, diced	7
Marinated salad:	
1½ cups sliced mushrooms	30
1 sliced green pepper	14
Marinade:	
1 tsp corn oil	42
1 to 2 tablespoons wine vinegar oregano, basil, or other herbs	2
	435 calories

The day's calories are now at 1037. You could almost feel full. You have been very good, so you are allowed to fill up on raw vegetables.

Now we come to day six. You'll have to get up a little early to cook this breakfast, but it is a new taste thrill, so it might be fun to do.

BREAKFAST

½ cup buckwheat cereal, cooked (called kasha or groats)	100
1 cup apple juice (the cereal can be cooked in the juice)	120
1 cup raspberries	72
	292 calories

LUNCH

3 ounces salmon, canned with bones	180
2 stalks celery, raw	14
1 carrot, raw	21
1 cup strawberries	50
	265 calories

DINNER

3 ounces pork loin chop, lean, broiled (eat lean part only)	150
1 sweet potato, baked with skin	155
Tossed green salad:	
½ head lettuce	30
10 endive leaves	5

2 tablespoons parsley or coriander	10
1 tablespoon sunflower seeds	80
Dressing:	
1 tablespoon sunflower oil,	
apple cider vinegar, kelp,	
tarragon	<u>120</u>
	550 calories

If you have made it through dinner, you have only taken in 1107 calories for these three meals. But don't blow the whole day because you have been so good. One ice cream cone will give you about 300 calories.

Here is an example of a low-calorie breakfast that is ready to eat when you get up. Fruit lovers take note.

BREAKFAST

You may use dried fruit, as is or stewed, or soaked in water overnight to leach out the sugar. Fresh fruit would serve as well and would be lower in calories.

(Dried fruit)		(Fresh fruit)	
⅓ cup prunes	80	2 med plums	66
⅓ cup apricots	130	3 apricots	55
⅓ cup peaches	<u>71</u>	1 med peach	<u>38</u>
	281 calories		159 calories

I know from experience, however, that I could not get through the morning on fruit alone; I would do better to eat nothing, or to have a piece of fruit every two hours to keep my blood sugar from sagging at midmorning. The fiber and the pectin in the fruit would slow the absorption of the sugar, so the above would be better than just juice or fruit sauce.

The following menus, for the seventh and eighth days, have about the same number of calories as the other days. You will notice that no food has been repeated more than once every four or five days. You should be getting an idea of how much food makes 300 to 400 calories. You should by now be able to get by on less sugar, fat, and salt. Your craving for the goodies is still there but you can control it.

BREAKFAST

2 biscuits shredded wheat	160
1 cup pineapple, diced or canned chunks in own juice	80
1 cup nonfat milk	88
	328 calories

LUNCH

2 corn tortillas (6-inch diameter)	110
1-ounce slice low-fat cheese (Mozzarella)	96
2 pieces jalapeño pepper (optional)	14
1 small bunch grapes	100
	320 calories

DINNER

1 lamb chop (2-ounce, lean part only)	120
1 medium potato with skin	100
2 tablespoons yogurt (low-fat) for potato	20
Sautéed vegetables:	
1 cup raw diced eggplant	100
1 sliced tomato	33

1 cup sliced mushrooms	20
½ tablespoon corn oil to sauté	63
	456 calories

The total calories so far for the three meals is 1104. If you can nibble on a few snacks between the meals to keep your blood sugar up and even, you should be able to stick to this diet. One tablespoon of walnuts is 42 calories. One raw green pepper is a nice, filling 14.

Try this for a change when you are trying to vary your breakfasts:

BREAKFAST

2 ounces turkey, ground (broiled) with a pinch of ground ginger	116
6 ounces prune juice	148
½ cantaloupe	58
	322 calories

LUNCH

Salad:

3 ounces tuna, water-packed	100
½ pound spinach	59

Dressing:

½ tablespoon olive oil	60
1 cup zucchini rounds, raw	25
1 banana	87
	331 calories

DINNER

4 ounces whitefish, broiled	176
1 cup borscht	54

Salad:

1 cucumber, sliced	31
3 olives, sliced	45
1 wedge watermelon (to be eaten at least an hour later)	<u>110</u>
	416 calories

This makes a total for the day of 1069. If you think you are getting cheated, you may try a few snacks like nuts and seeds. But don't eat everything at once. Remember to separate the fruit from the protein, or you will have gas, gas, gas.

If this Phase Four of Dr. Smith's Low-Stress Weight Control Diet is just not as satisfactory as the promise of a few pages ago, Phase Five should be launched. It could be the best thing you ever did for yourself.

PHASE FIVE: PRACTICALLY IMPOSSIBLE TO LOSE

The thyroid gland may be your noncompliant, passive obstructionist, the stubborn, willful opponent of your efforts to control your body. It just may not be working as it should. Thyroid hypofunction is a fairly common mechanism that produces lethargy, weight increase, and sloppy metabolic function. It is placed fifth in progression on the way to optimal weight control because the preceding phases may have corrected a faulty thyroid gland. Thyroid function depends upon the B vitamins and requires iodine and protein as raw materials to make the hormones. The thyroid gland needs thyroid hormone as much as the rest of the body cells do. The thyroid needs thyroid to help the thyroid make thyroid. One must be healthy to be healthy.

Thyroid hormone regulates the metabolism of each cell of the body. An infant deprived of it becomes short and retarded, a cretin. According to Dr. Broda Barnes, author of *Hypothyroidism: The Unsuspected Illness,*[10] low thyroid function can mimic just about every disease known to man, even hyperthyroidism. In medical school, we were taught to consider, at least, the possibility of hypothyroidism in lethargic, dull patients who had thick, waxy, dry skin and complained of being cold when everyone else was comfortable.

Dr. Barnes feels it serves no useful purpose to await these symptoms. The doctor believes that taking the temperature for five minutes orally or in the armpit before getting out of bed in the morning is more accurate than the rather complicated laboratory blood test for T3 and T4 (see page 66). The thermometer should then read 97.8° to 98.2°. If it consistently registers in the low 97s or 96s, it surely means the thyroid is not being produced in sufficient amounts to do the work of the body, or that the thyroid hormones are sufficient but the receptor sites of that particular person's body need more thyroid to make them respond. The basal metabolic rate, the hum of the billions of cells doing their work like a busy ant colony, all add up to a temperature that is standard for the human machine.

When humans attempt to fast, or when they take in fewer calories than the body has been used to, the thyroid gland cuts back on production as a conservation measure. This is one reason why people become angry with their bodies; they do not realize that when they cut back from 2000 to 1000 calories a day, the thyroid usually slows down its thyroxine production. The basal metabolism is slowed. Fat is not burned up as readily.

A checkup with the doctor would be prudent at about this time. The ovaries work with the thyroid, so problems with these glands might have a debilitating effect on the thyroid. If one carefully words the complaints ("cold," "dry," "tired," "constipated"), the doctor should be aware that those words suggest

10. New York: Thomas Y. Crowell, 1976.

the blood chemistry tests for T3 and T4. A high cholesterol level in the blood often means low thyroid function.

If the T3 and T4 are low, you may find that thyroid hormone replacement will very nicely take care of your metabolic problems. You should now be able to dump some weight easily and efficiently. You can say, "I knew it was glandular, all along." You might notice that the following symptoms will disappear also: fatigue, headaches, repeated infections, eczema, cold and dry skin, menstrual disturbances, constipation, loss of memory, inability to concentrate, coarse hair, and depression. The standard treatment is Armour Thyroid, tablets prepared from fresh, desiccated animal thyroid glands. Some object that these doses cannot be standardized, but most nutritionists believe that synthetic substitutes just do not work. A 1-grain tablet is taken every morning for seven to ten days while the patient monitors his or her temperature. If no response in energy and temperature is noted, 2 grains are taken every morning for a week. These 1-grain increments are made every week until the temperature is running about 98° in the morning and the fatigue is less and the hands are warm. This slow increase in the number of pills should prevent an overdose—which would not be serious, although the effects—rapid heart, softness of the stools, insomnia—might frighten one. These are hyperthyroid symptoms. The dose should be reduced if these symptoms appear. Now everything should be set to permit an almost effortless weight loss. You should feel good.

Some people find that the thyroid gland hormone has to be continued for the rest of their lives. Some need it only to get started (for one to three months) and then the dose can be reduced once the body is "balanced." Some are concerned that "needless" or "inappropriate" thyroid use will so suppress the normal hormone output that the gland will atrophy and the victim will forever need replacement therapy. Not so. Repeated therapy with thyroid hormone in conditions of questionable need have taught us that the normal thyroid will bounce back to full functioning capacity sixty days after any suppressive effects of inappropriate therapy. So a therapeutic trial is worthwhile based on the low temperature readings.

But what do you do if the T3 and T4 show up in the normal range and your temperature suggests low thyroid hormone function (production is okay, but the cells do not respond to that level)? You plead with your doctor for a prescription, but he or she feels that the blood test is the only valid way to determine hormone function.

Before you threaten the doctor, here are ideas to try: Tyrosine, an amino acid, combines with iodine to make thyroxine, the thyroid hormone. You need both of them in your diet along with copper to supply the gland so the hormone can be synthesized. We need at least 100 to 150 mcg a day of iodine; seafood and seaweed are our best sources. Clams, kelp, shrimp, haddock, halibut, oysters, salmon, and sardines carry more iodine than most other foods. (If you are using iodized salt, it is probably not necessary to supplement your iodine.) Copper is in oysters, brazil nuts, and soy lecithin. Tyrosine is in lean meats, whole grains, and legumes. You can consume tyrosine tablets, 1000 mg per day, and get enough to do the job.

Some healthy foods will slow down the action of the thyroid in some people. Brussels sprouts, broccoli, cauliflower, cabbage, and related vegetables may be suppressing the gland. Muscle meats, peanuts, and soybeans may dampen the function of the thyroid. Excessive doses of vitamin A and iodine may slow down the thyroid activity. The nitrates in some meats impair the synthesis of thyroxine. Fluoride is an enzyme toxin.

These herbs drunk as teas will benefit the thyroid: golden seal, myrrh, black cohosh. Exercise can help the thyroid.

If everything points to a sluggish thyroid as your problem, you may have to find a sympathetic doctor.

In cases where the thyroid-replacement method of Phase

Five proves helpful, along with the good diet, the B-vitamin assistance, some exercise, and the elimination of the foods to which one is sensitive, many find it possible gradually to reduce their thyroid therapy after a few months—depending upon the symptoms and the morning temperature, of course.

PHASE SIX: IMPOSSIBLE TO LOSE WITHOUT A STOMACH-STAPLING OR INTESTINAL BYPASS OPERATION

Hold it! A couple more things to try. Surgery is so final, so end-point-like. If you are stuck with minimal weight loss and just cannot budge the bulge, you are entitled to anger and depression. I would suggest a re-evaluation from a doctor and perhaps a visit to an endocrinologist just for an opinion. If the consensus is that it is all in your head, the hypnotist, the psychiatrist, and the acupuncturist would be the next most appropriate sources of help. A nutritionist can be invaluable. I am assuming that somewhere along the line, or even before you arrived at Phase One, you tried Weight Watchers or the Diet Service plan or some other local or franchised group that relies heavily on a program of mutual support.

Many of these programs are successful because they change their clients' eating styles. These new habits slow the gobblers and the gulpers. If you have to chew each bite thirty times (Dr. Fletcher said that back in 1929), then the blood sugar might rise high enough before the next bite to slow the eater's enthusiasm for more food.

Consider whether your absorption problem might really be a dental problem. Malocclusion or decayed and missing teeth will cut down the ingestion of roughage foods, seeds, nuts, and raw vegetables. These people tend to seek puddings, cereals, and soft, often highly caloric foods. Dentists have told pediatricians for years to prohibit their patients from eating liquid calories (soft drinks, fruit juices). If children consume many liquid calories while they are growing, the jaws do not get exercised and an underdeveloped lower jaw could be the result. We are supposed to be drinking just water.

The tendency to osteoporosis and its associated missing teeth seems to be taking its toll at earlier ages because of the low levels of minerals in our foods and the high intake of animal protein, sugar, and soft drinks. These items provide the body with a disproportionate amount of phosphorus which triggers the parathyroid glands in the neck to secrete their hormone. This pulls the calcium out of the bones to balance the phosphorus. The calcium runs out in the urine, leading to demineralization of the bones. Calcium loss between ages twenty-five years to seventy-five years can be as much as 50 percent of the skeleton. It is average in our country to be edentulous by the age of sixty years. Poor dentition can contribute to poor weight management. We get the sugar from foods more quickly when we eat low-roughage, low-fiber, and low-pectin foods. Instead of the apple, we eat the sauce—or, even worse, the juice. Quick sugar in our foods enhances the storage problem. We are growing up to become a nation of toothless fatties with narrow jaws. The pain and stress of the temporomandibular joint syndrome is partially based on lifelong dietary habits. The dental route, enabling you to eat the high-roughage, more lowly absorbed foods, may be your path to weight control.

Do not discount the possibility of candidiasis, "the twentieth-century disease." A yeast infection of the intestinal tract, its symptoms are multiple and varied. Indeed, it is felt that if a person has symptoms in at least three body systems the yeast toxin is responsible. If you have distension and bloating, lethargy, chemical sensitivities, cystitis (repeated bladder infections), and food cravings, you are probably suffering from this fungus and some treatment would be called for. Yeast infection can explain arthritis, gastritis, colitis, diarrhea alternating with constipation, headaches, depression, sinusitis, endometriosis—whatever. It can make a person feel so rotten that he or she does not exercise and may eat poorly.

The condition masks as hypoglycemia because of periodic attacks of weakness and adverse reactions to sugar. It simulates food allergies because bread, beer, cheese, and wine make the sufferer sick, weak, and gaseous. The consistent complaints are fatigue—bone-tired weariness—and memory loss. Dr. C. Orian Truss, who has made us all aware of the ubiquity of the condition, says these people cannot remember what they had for lunch the day before.[11]

Usually the victims are women, but it can affect anyone whose immune system has been weakened by antibiotics (treatment for acne, sore throat, bladder infections), cortisonelike drugs (for severe allergies, hives, asthma, poison oak), contraceptive pills, and replacement hormones (estrogen) in postmenopausal women. Frequent episodes of herpes seem to characterize these victims. Stress seems to be a consistent triggering event. The immune system is so involved with the yeast, it has little ability to control the ordinary infections and allergies.

The candidiasis yeast prefers chocolate, sweets, grains, dairy products, fruit juices, and nuts. Many sufferers have cravings for fermented, pickled, smoked, or dried foods. It is common for female victims to feel they *must* have these goodies in the week before their periods.

When foods have been produced by fermentation processes they trigger symptoms and reduce the body's immune system further. The following should be avoided until the yeast infestation is under control: commercial breads, pastries, beer, wine, commercial soups, barbecued potato chips, dry roasted nuts, soy sauce, and anything with a vinegar base, which includes many salad dressings. All cheeses, dried fruits, bacon, honey, maple

11. C. Orian Truss, M.D., *The Missing Diagnosis*, published 1983 by C. O. Truss, 2614 Highland Avenue, Birmingham, AL 35205.

syrup, and nuts are loaded with mold and cross-react with the candida. Eating fruits and fruit juices will feed the yeast; these things must be avoided for a while. Teas and dried spices are other foods that accumulate mold.

Treatment with nystatin, an antiyeast medicine, is standard. Until the yeast is under better control, the diet should be limited to fresh animal protein and vegetables. Yogurt, acidophilus milk, garlic, and taheebo tea are helpful in suppressing the yeast growth; start with quarter-cup of the tea twice daily and slowly build up to one cup three times a day.[12] Some benefit is obtained with the use of 6 tablespoons of olive oil daily. Biotin, 1000 mg daily, might help.

Behavior modification has been helpful in retraining people to have a different attitude toward food and eating. Along with that training, people should understand the physiology of the stomach. Eating the protein first helps to make the most of the acid digestion. The little bit of fat that naturally accompanies most meat serves to slow down the emptying time of the stomach; hunger is assuaged. We should be nice to the pancreas and nibble frequently on foods that would not cause a sudden rise in the blood sugar. If we eat foods that nourish the adrenals we might not notice stress so acutely. Taking all the proper vitamins and minerals will keep the intestinal lining cells functioning. Exercise and the B-complex vitamins will increase the effectiveness of the mitochondria which burn up fat. The diet program *will not work* without an exercise program.

12. William G. Crook, M.D., *The Yeast Connection* (Jackson, Tenn.: Professional Books, 1983). Also, C. D. Hawley, M.D., and B. W. Stratford, M.D., office newsletter, Livermore, California.

6

Diets for Life's Stressful Times

Each era of our life has its own set of stresses—from the moment we are conceived to the day we lose the partner of a lifetime. It would be good if we could get out of the stressful situation, but most of the time we just have to live through it and do what we can to stay healthy in body and mind. We have to eat and exercise prudently so the body can more easily maintain homeostasis.

Remember this important rule of weight management and stress control: It is just as easy to eat the right things as the wrong things—and more pleasurable too.

Where It All Begins

Nothing puts a human being together better than a happy, healthy nine months in the womb. It would seem to obvious to need stating, but where would we be without the time spent inside our mothers? Nowhere! The quality of that intrauterine time greatly determines the potential future well-being or ill-being of that child.

The medical teaching used to be that because the mother's body is so large and the fertilized egg is so microscopically small, the parasite could extract everything it needed—for the first few months of life anyway. But now we know that the fast-multiplying cells need to be bathed in protein, fat, carbohydrate, water, oxygen, hormones, vitamins, and minerals. If these things are not in the bloodstream, going to the uterus, the baby will not get them. Moreover, if the baby does not get them at critical times in the formation of certain organs, a defect is produced that will have lifelong effects. Protein in abundance is needed in the early months to fulfill the requirements of the rapidly growing brain. A deficiency in those early weeks will prevent the fetus from getting all the nerve cells it is supposed to get for optimum cerebral function, and this defect is irreversible. For example, it has been well established that an insufficient amount of folic acid (a B vitamin) in the early weeks of some pregnancies will produce a spine defect in the babies, leaving them paralyzed from the waist down.

I see milk allergies in babies if the allergic tendency is in the family and the mother drank a quart of milk daily during the nine months. She needs the calcium, but this daily impact of dairy products seems to predispose the sensitive ones to a milk allergy. Many of these mothers will try to nurse the offspring thus sensitized, but the cow's milk she consumes will be present in her breast milk in sufficient quantity to upset the baby. The mother assumes something is wrong with *her* milk, stops nursing, and puts the baby on cow's milk. The baby becomes more disturbed, and because the mother has dried up, the baby must now make the round of soy, goat's, and lamb-based milks, often becoming sensitive to each of these. The mother should have known. *Her* mother might have known. The doctor is the authority. Where was he?

Vitamin C supplements have been shown to reduce the

allergic tendency in the baby and cut down the time it takes to deliver the child (a long, difficult delivery could be a stress sufficient to precipitate an allergy). The suggested dose for the pregnant woman is 1000 mg of vitamin C daily for the first three months, 2000 to 4000 mg of vitamin C daily for the middle three months, and 4 to 6 grams daily for the final trimester, depending on bowel tolerance, of course. Loose stools suggest that one should reduce the dose. The mother should be exercising daily, taking breathing classes, and, most importantly, she should be surrounded with supportive, empathetic friends and relatives— even if they have to be paid to be there. (Like a psychiatrist?)

In my patients, I have seen an increased incidence of allergies in children born following a pregnancy in which the mother was stressed. If you, Mother, are able to think ahead, you should try to become pregnant at a time when you are ready for the fifteen years of the PTA, and you are in love with the man who fathers your child, and you have a nest, and you have some energy for your career and the burdens of the uterine load. It *makes* a difference. You don't have to do a Rorschach or a Minnesota Multiphasic Personality Test on your partner, but it would be nice to have someone who is interested, tender, thoughtful, and who doesn't hit you.

You should avoid stressful situations while carrying your baby. If your job is a stress and you feel it, it would be best to quit, because that feeling is also affecting the baby. Stress tends to exhaust the adrenals and this leads to allergies and an impaired immune system. It would be a good idea to live in a home with comfortable people who are happy and proud that you are pregnant. It *is* important. Negative feelings during the pregnancy may produce an unhappy, sickly child who will be reared with difficulty.

No sugar, no white flour, no cigarettes, no alcohol, and no drugs, if at all possible, are the basic prohibitions to improve the environment of the fetus. You should eat only nourishing foods. Whole grains, fruits, vegetables cooked as little as possible, plenty of protein, calcium, and magnesium seem to be of first priority. Aim for a 30-pound gain for the nine months. Try to rotate your diet; do not eat the same food more frequently than every four days. This advice is especially important for the families with allergies. Use the vitamin C as indicated above. Get calcium (1000 to 2000 mg) and magnesium (750 to 1000 mg) daily from supplements and don't drink milk or eat dairy products every day; daily consumption of these common allergens may predispose the sensitive ones to a milk allergy.

Diet for an Infant

Don't let your mother feed you anything other than breast milk for the first six to ten months of your life. Breast-feeding significantly cuts the incidence of allergies and infections. If you get cramps, nausea, phlegm, a cough, or a rash despite the breast-feeding, it means your mother is eating something to which you are allergic (cow's milk, wheat, egg, corn, soy, whatever). Smile at her while you are nursing so she will get some real enjoyment out of the nursing; it isn't just for you, you know. Suck vigorously and try to sleep longer during the night than during the day and she will love you for it. (She will be able to brag to her friends, also.) Insist on nursing for a year, or better, for two years. You will have a better jaw line and more even teeth when you grow up. It may prevent the need for orthodontia and may reduce your chances of developing the painful temporomandibular joint syndrome when you are older.

If your mother really tried her best to nurse you but there were things in the way, don't hold a grudge. Raw goat's milk might be the next best mammalian milk to try. If your folks know the goat and it agrees with you, well and good. If you have trouble with that, then raw cow's milk might be okay, but, again, your folks should know and trust the cow. If neither of these two agrees with you, then maybe the next best one to try would be Similac, Enfamil, or SMA; all seem about the same. After a while they can use the one with added iron, so there will be less need to hurry the introduction of solid foods. Remember, though, Mom's milk is best.

If they attempt to push solids down your throat before you are six months old, fight them off; spit up, throw up, and let the gruel run down your chin—but smile while you are doing it. (Some kids get screamed at for blowing food at their parents.) You have to let them know that you are too young and your intestinal tract is not efficient enough to break down the non–breast-milk foods into their small, nonallergenic amino acids, fatty acids, and simple carbohydrates. When incompletely digested foods are absorbed, the body considers them foreign substances and the immune system produces antibodies against them. You may become sensitized to foods when they are introduced too early and you may never outgrow that problem.

Allergies in the family should encourage your parents to delay the early feeding of solids. The only valid reason for the solids is to prevent the cow's-milk anemia that is common in infants who drink only whole cow's milk. (Calves can absorb the iron from raw cow's milk; humans cannot.) If your mother is on a good diet, you will get enough iron from her milk despite your rapid growth. But just nursing, nursing, nursing may be boring for her, although it is the best way to feed you. She might like some relief from your need for constant oral gratification. Besides, your dad might like to do something for you other than just changing and cuddling you. But the switch to solids should not be done until you are ready for it.

Your parents push solids down your reluctant gullet because they think that a large caloric load might get the noncompliant one (you) to sleep through the night. Every once in a while that works, but the usual reason for night wakefulness is some gas going sideways or a milk allergy or a reaction to something your mother ate the day before that got into her breast milk. Some of you infants are restless at night because you are low in calcium and magnesium; this is a common deficiency because your mother did not get enough during the pregnancy and you are outgrowing the supply. Sometimes your parents know no other solution than to feed you, which might be the reason why you will grow up to be overweight. (A calm-the-kid-with-food pattern often is established in infancy.)

Calcium and magnesium in 100- to 200-mg doses at bedtime might just do the trick for you. You might sleep through and not notice a wet diaper or a wrinkle in the sheet or a pea under the mattress. If you are a thumb-sucker or a bed-rocker it might dawn on them that you need those minerals; not every unacceptable bit of behavior is due to insecurity. Zinc and manganese are helpful also. If you have to suck your thumb to get to sleep, try to quit the habit by taking minerals before age five years, because it can distort your jaw line.

Your mother might find that when you are nine to ten months old you are not so desperately hungry and she can poke some of the solids into you when you are smiling at her. Make sure she starts you on the ones less likely to cause sensitivities. The foods that are eaten frequently by your family are the ones to which you are likely to become sensitive. Cow's milk, of course, would be number one. Then there are corn, soy, wheat, eggs, citrus, peanuts, shellfish, and all the rest. Most people are not allergic to rutabagas, or turnips, so Mother should start you on those (ugh, sorry). Pears are better fruits to start with than citrus, apples, or peaches. Barley is less of a sensitizer than wheat or rice. Yellow vegetables are usually less likely to cause allergic reactions than the green ones like peas and beans. Try to spit out corn, soy, and the other no-nos listed above. Rice is a common allergen for Orientals, and corn is the most common allergen for Mexicans. After your first year, some of these would be safe to try, but aim to have them only every four days.

Mom should not offer you calorie-dense food (i.e., cream, pudding, jams, jellies, white bread, soda crackers). These things could set you up for future obesity. In one study,[1] the number of lipid cells increased in all infants until age two years. Children who did not become obese had a decrease in lipid content of the cells after the age of one year. After the age of two years, their lipid cells became smaller than they were at the age of one year. However, those infants who grew up to become obese had an increase in the lipid content of cells in the second year.

I would recommend that you be given mashed banana sprinkled with some B-complex vitamins from a capsule. It isn't the greatest taste in the world, but it is good for you. Your mom can alternate that with some minerals given the same way.

Try not to eat the same thing every day. Allergies will develop less easily if the foods are rotated every four to five days. One of the quickest ways to let your folks know that something is disgusting or nauseating or that it hurts is to throw it up on them.

It may be difficult to let your folks know that you enjoy your family and are comfortable. If you are basically cheerful—you laugh and smile more than you cry and frown—then you are probably doing great. But frequent aches and pains, inability to go to sleep easily, night wakefulness, and many colds and allergies may make your parents feel inadequate. Some parents *should* feel inadequate and guilty about the way they are feeding you and taking care of you. Your parents may bring you to the doctor looking for some reason for your irritability and discomfort.

Your parents and your doctor cannot guess what is the matter with you, because all you seem to do is lie there and cry or whimper or whine. Nothing specific. But if you notice things too easily, or jump when the phone rings, or cry when the vacuum cleaner is on, and if you are ticklish and goosey, they should be able to figure out that you are probably low in calcium and magnesium.

1. Jerome L. Knittle, M.D., "Metabolic query: Why do fat kids have fatter fat cells?," *Journal of the American Medical Association*, vol. 239, no. 17 (28 April 1978), p. 1730.

It is important that someone figure out what your body is telling you (and, we hope, them), because allergies and the inability to disregard stress often set up the biochemical mechanism that leads to psychosomatic diseases and, of course, to obesity. All pediatricians are supposed to know about the evils of feeding solids early and its risk of developing allergies that may be a permanent part of the person's physiology. For one thing, food allergies can lead to obesity.

Diet If You Are About Eighteen Months to Two Years of Age

You are supposed to cut down on your food intake and start to whine a lot. It really gets to your parents. They *know* that if you would just eat a little better, you would feel better, and if you would feel better, you would eat better. They think they are dealing with a case of anorexia. But stick with it. Small amounts frequently. Nibble, nibble. Pediatricians get extra business from kids this age because the parents feel their child must have mono or TB or anemia to account for the terrible noncompliance.

Try to show a preference for steamed vegetables, whole grains, fruits, seeds, and nuts. The latter might choke you, so insist on nut butters (natural, without sugar or salt, of course) spread on whole-grain bread. This is nutritious and tastes good. Because of your poor appetite but continued growth, you must eat foods of high nutritional density: a bite of fish or chicken (drop the skin on the floor for the dog), barely cooked vegetables (raw if your molars are working), fruit (don't let your folks foist the juices on you, because you need the pectin, the fiber, and the cellulose in the whole fruit), oatmeal or other whole-grain cereals, and milk—but only every fourth day because it's such a common allergen.

You can see your dilemma: you need protein, calcium, magnesium, vitamins C and B, and iron, but you eat next to nothing. If you drink enough milk to get your daily calcium requirement (the Dairy Council says you should have a quart a day to get the 800 mg of calcium you need, since the body absorbs only about half of what is swallowed), you will have taken in enough calories to last twenty-four hours but virtually no iron and no roughage. So you get anemic. It might be worthwhile to take some supplements of calcium, vitamin C, B complex, and a little folic acid just to stay healthy. If you have trouble sleeping at night, take the calcium and magnesium at bedtime. Children and adults need about 1000 mg of calcium and 750 mg or more of magnesium daily. Zinc (20 to 30 mg and manganese (5 to 10 mg) would help you if you are crabby and fussy and cannot relax and sleep at night.

Diet If You Are Four to Six Years of Age

I hope you are starting some excellent health habits which will become so strong that you won't be able to deviate from them all the rest of your life. Brushing and flossing your teeth, not eating sugar except on birthdays and Halloween (and then only a little if you really have to), exercising, breathing deeply, getting the proper amount of sleep, and swallowing the required nutrients for your body. We need water, protein, carbohydrates, and some fats. The vitamins and minerals are supposed to be provided by the foods, but refining, processing, marketing, and cooking have depleted many of the important nutrients. The impoverished topsoil does not have the full quota of minerals, so the marketed fruits, vegetables, and grains do not always contain the promised minerals. I therefore urge you to eat food as wholesome and unprocessed as possible; but, in addition, establishing a daily supplement program is prudent insurance.

Vitamin C, 500 to 5000 mg, is to be taken daily depending upon the consistency of your bowel movements. Increase the dose by 500 mg every day until the stools get just a little soft (usually between 500 to 5000 mg); stay right there. C is important if you have allergies or repeated infections.

The B complex tastes like moldy dirt and most people your age cannot swallow pills or capsules with ease. Some can swallow brewer's yeast if it is combined with other foods like orange juice, peanut butter, or a mashed banana. Try to get at least 10 to 20 mg of each of the Bs, plus a few micrograms of B_{12} and 0.4 mg of folic acid.

An all-purpose mineral tablet or capsule would be worth taking. Zinc, manganese, chromium, iron, molybdenum should be in there. Use of a multi-mineral without copper as the food and water now seems to supply us with a sufficient amount. Can you grind it up into a powder and then stick it into some food?

Cod-liver oil has vitamin A and D in it and is important for your skin and bones. The unconcentrated oil might be better (if you can get used to the taste), because it contains some essential fatty acids.

Calcium (1000 mg) and magnesium (750 mg or more) are best taken at bedtime; they will help you sleep better. You can take them in pill, powder, or liquid form.

The whole idea here is to give you some reliable guidelines so you can maintain your health and enjoy your life and even contribute something to others or to the world in general. All great people started out as children.

Many children (and adults) simply do not feel good, but they have nothing with which to compare this feeling because they can only live inside the body they "have on" now. Some feel good one day and bad the next. Children get headaches and stomach aches, get very tired, wake up in the middle of the night frightened, have muscle cramps, get nervous, cannot stand loud noises, and hate to be tickled.

You have to become an expert in the way your body works; you will be living in it for the rest of your life. Maybe you don't know it yet, but the wrong oil and cheap gas will wreck the engine of your car. Just the same way, your body will get sick or weak or not grow properly if it is fed too much sugar and processed food.

This book is supposed to help you figure out what your body is trying to tell you. Learning what the various symptoms mean should be part of the education you get from your mother and father and the school system. All your life you will be trying to understand how to be comfortable inside that body of yours. Get an early start.

Diet for the First Day of Anything—
Especially Nursery School, Kindergarten, or Grade School

This is a stressful time. You will be meeting new adults, and making new friends. They will expect you to fit into *their* routine of sitting still, paying attention, working with unfamiliar toys, and going to the bathroom when *they* want you to and you don't need to (or it is already too late). There will be noise and some confusion. If you feel scared, you will get it fixed in your mind that school is a dangerous place, and that attitude could color the rest of your academic encounters. That scared feeling is caused by adrenalin in your bloodstream which is secreted by the adrenal glands when you find yourself in new situations. When your blood sugar falls, the adrenalin is *really* squirted into your system. And that may happen if you eat sugary foods or foods to which you are allergic.

I realize that the excitement of anticipating the day may nauseate you to the point of anorexia, but you should try to get some kind of long-term energy source down to your stomach. But *no* sugary cereal or chocolate milk or Tang or sweet roll; they make the adrenalin flow faster. Try whole-grain toast spread with old-fashioned peanut butter and topped with a dollop of applesauce. One cooked egg. I sometimes put a hard-boiled egg in my pocket and eat it at a convenient time later on in the morning. Maybe your mother is standing over you scowling because she is not satisfied with the way your clothes, hair, and nails look. Smile and reassure her that you won't be a blot on the family reputation, and before you go off to school put a piece of cheese in your pocket or a handful of almonds in your book bag. Eat a little bit of the cheese or an almond every twenty minutes or so. It should keep your blood sugar and your spirits up. Sometimes it is better to go hungry rather than eat one of those sugary breakfast cereals or a sweet drink or a doughnut. So much for your blood sugar.

Some calcium, perhaps 250 to 300 mg in powder form or a suspension, should help you settle into the class routine with equanimity. It provides calmness without the doped feeling that accompanies tranquilizers. About 100 mg of magnesium (like ¼ teaspoon of Epsom salts) along with the calcium makes the latter more effective. If you have a startle reflex or overreact to noise, these should help you stay undistracted by the strange sounds in the classroom. Be careful with the magnesium; too much might force you to spend most of the first day sitting on the toilet.

Vitamin C, at about the 1000-mg level, might be a good thing to help your immune system, since you will be exposed to some new varieties of viruses and germs. If you even *think* the first day is stressful, your immune system can be weakened. The vitamin C can help you be comfortable acquiring antibodies against the various pathogens that will be exhaled onto you; you will get minor cold symptoms and occasional fevers but you need not be devastated.

It is important to remember that all the other children in your class or school are going through the same first-day tension. It can be a stress. Some notice the stress more than others. It may be the first time in your life that you have been separated from your parents. You notice that your heart is pounding in your chest; you can feel it against your ribs. You may notice sweaty palms, blurred vision, and the hair rising on the back of your neck. Your mouth may be dry and there may be a sinking feeling in the pit of your stomach. You may be lightheaded and close to fainting. If you breathe deeply and frequently you could pass out. Manganese, 10 mg, A.M. and P.M., will help.

These feelings that you notice are the result of the fluctuation of the sugar level in your bloodstream. This level will rise rapidly in many of those who eat quick, sugary foods. The body does not like sudden changes, so the pancreas releases insulin to drive the blood sugar down. If the person overproduces insulin the blood sugar level may fall too fast and too far. To compensate for this the adrenal glands produce adrenalin, assuming that your blood sugar would not be falling so fast unless you were fighting off a tiger. The adrenalin flow is a reaction of the nervous system which has perceived a threat, a surprise, or a difficult situation. But, as we have seen, the adrenalin also flows when the blood sugar drops from the effects of the diet. The adrenalin is the body's safeguard to preserve the status quo: it brings sugar out of storage in the liver and it helps the body be alert during a crisis.

The scary feelings that this adrenalin causes in your body can make you want to fly away or fight or hide. When you are in a room with other kids and you notice these paniclike symptoms, but the others seem calm *and there is no obvious threat,* it is called an inappropriate anxiety attack. It serves no useful purpose; it's a big waste of time and energy. If you get these attacks frequently, it means you are eating sugar or some food to which you are allergic, and that you are unable to disregard the room, the environment, and the world.

Take some sodium or potassium bicarbonate (for example, Alka-Seltzer Gold); it will neutralize the acidosis that is part of the twisted biochemistry that has you in its grip. You need a diet change and a better source of calcium, magnesium, and B complex.

Diet for Going to a Party or to the Dentist
or Any Other Stressful Event

You might find the following helpful if you are applying for a job, or if you want to be cool on a date. Dr. William Philpott has found,[2] and the American College of Allergists has stated, that 80 percent of people who have food allergies also have low blood sugar.[3] The following combination of nutrients will keep the blood sugar even, thus preventing the characteristic adrenalin release and the resultant, awful, impending-doom feeling ("Let's get out of here!"). This usually will preclude the release of adrenalin despite the ingestion of sugary or allergenic foods.

Calcium, 500 to 1000 mg

Magnesium, 500 to 1000 mg

Don't overdo the calcium and magnesium; too much of these may act as a downer.

B_6, 50 to 100 mg, or a potent B complex

Vitamin C, 500 to 1000 mg

Plus some food that releases energy such as protein (meat, fish, egg), complex carbohydrate (vegetable or grain), or some safe fat (nuts or seeds).

The idea here is that the latter food would keep the blood sugar even and the neocortex energized (memory, rational thought, and humaneness are centered there), and the calcium, magnesium, C, and B would serve to fuel the adrenals, the first organs to be kicked when stress is perceived.

2. William H. Philpott, M.D., and Dwight K. Kalita, Ph.D., *Brain Allergies: The Psycho-nutrient Connection* (New Canaan, Conn.: Keats Publishing Co., 1980).

3. When blood sugar drops, adrenalin is released and the brain is not nourished.

(On the day of writing this I went to an important meeting where we discussed plans affecting my future. Although I had had a good breakfast with eggs, whole wheat toast, sausage, and some fruit, I could not refuse the muffins and zucchini bread offered at the coffee break. I did not want to offend our hostess, and I do love those baked things. But when it came time to make my presentation, I found I was on edge. Sure, that's only normal, but I have been in other tense situations where I did not notice the adrenalin flowing. Also, I had been without my B complex for four days. It *does* make a difference.)

The point is that with a little planning we can think ahead and protect our body and preserve the homeostasis. (Better to say that we can help the body preserve its homeostasis.) The body does not like physiological and biochemical changes—or at least it feels it must respond with hormonal secretions to reverse the upset. If we do not provide the nutrients necessary to replenish these exhausted glands and cells, a symptom or sign will develop. If you like having asthma or eczema, or migraine, or colitis, okay, but it seems useless, without purpose, inappropriate. I am sure many of us seek out drugs, alcohol, or tobacco because the body is an uncomfortable place in which to live when the adrenalin, histamine, and other chemicals are released during these stressful times.

I have been delighted with the ease and safety of baby shots (DPT, measles-mumps-rubella, polio drops) when the infant or child gets the C, calcium, and B complex on the day before, the day of, and the day after the administration of these vaccines. I have been impressed with the lack of reaction to the DPT especially if I give 0.5 cc of a B complex with C injected in one muscle when I give the DPT in another muscle.

Diet for the Five- to Eighteen-Year-Old (or More)—Who Is Having Trouble in School (Slow Reading, Poor Memory, "Not Working Up to Potential")

It is especially important as you grow up to gain insight into the clues your body is displaying. It is trying to get your attention so you'll do something about them.

My milk allergy (or better, my sensitivity to homogenized/pasteurized milk) tried to let me know there was something wrong by first giving me ear infections and a mastoid infection at age five years. Then there was the bed-wetting that dragged on till age thirteen, to be replaced with nosebleeds that have gone on forever. It was as if my body could not get my attention with one symptom or sign so it tried another, until finally in my twenties, I realized *Aha!* it was the milk. All those wasted, embarrassing years.

Your body is unique; there is none other quite like it. (Mister Rogers says you're special.) And you are the expert in "reading" it. You should know especially that if you have mood swings, if you are a Jekyll-and-Hyde type or a Terrible-Tempered Mr. Bangs, then you are having trouble with your blood sugar or an excess of adrenalin in your body or insulin in your brain. You do not—I repeat—you do not have to assume it is a psychiatric disorder. Your brain is misfiring because of poor or inadequate fuel.

It is very difficult to understand what is going on, because the part of the brain that should have judgment and insight is not working during these episodes of spaciness or *non compos mentis* or depression. If friends or your teacher or your parents are not observant enough to see the hourly or daily fluctuations, this is what you must do: Try to summarize on Friday what the week was like and what you ate each day. Could you read on Monday and not on Tuesday? Were you angry on Wednesday and not on Thursday? Did your handwriting change from legible to illegible between Friday A.M. and Friday P.M.? (Years ago I noticed that after a stress-filled day and a poor lunch my hand-writing was so illegible that I could not write out a prescription for the patient in my office. I would say to the mother, "I'll call the pharmacist; that way you won't have to wait when you get to the drugstore." I prayed that the harassed pharmacist had had a better day than I and that he was typing the Rx as I talked to him. A good druggist will read the Rx back over the phone to me, to see if we both have it right.)

If you have academic difficulties consistently every day, then your breakfast is to blame (doughnut and coffee with sugar?), or you are low in the B complex (not getting enough from im-poverished food). To blame the school system or a poor teacher is a cop-out. Remember, good and bad days or good and bad hours are *nutritional*, not emotional or psychiatric, in origin.

Try this tack if they drag you into the principal's office: "The fluorescent lights make me sick; they are not full-spectrum, are they?" (See the light research by John Ott.[4]) I have also found that cheerfulness is a good survival technique. Try pretending to be in a good mood—sometimes it works and can change your whole day. Other people usually can't be stern with you if you're in a good mood—and it can be contagious!

See the Dr. Smith's Diet, Phase Two, for your specific nutritional program.

Diet for a Girl Ten to Fifteen Years of Age or a Boy About Twelve to Eighteen Years of Age Who Is Growing Rapidly

This is surely a stressful time for you. You have some oily skin and pimples showing, the genitals are enlarging and twing-ing, and pubic hair is growing. You are trying to sort out your life and the problems with school and your family, and then your

---

4. *Health and Light* (Old Greenwich, Conn.: Devin-Adair Co., 1973).

friends suggest that you try drugs, alcohol, marijuana, and cigarettes. You are tempted because these are your friends and it
seems cool. What you may not realize is that they are just as
frightened by the bodily changes and sexual urges as you are.
You will have some anxiety-laden years ahead, but no matter
what lifestyle you want to adopt for the next few days or months,
you have to nourish the growth and the nervous system that
must absorb the stress. A good diet can help with both. Try the
following for just a month and see if you feel more cheerful and
smooth and even. Little or no sugar, please.

Only one hamburger or fast-food meal a week. Eat whole
grains, seeds, nuts, vegetables, fruit, salads, small amounts of
meat, chicken, and fish. Try to have dairy products only once
every four to five days. Do the following routine every day for
a month:

Vitamin C, 1000 mg (take more if sick or allergic)

B complex: 50 mg of each of the Bs; folic acid, 0.4 mg;
B_{12}, 100 mcg

Vitamin A, 30,000 units

Zinc, 60 mg

Calcium, 1000 mg, and magnesium, at least 750 mg, at
bedtime

Then stop the routine for a month and see if you feel worse. If
so, it is a sign that you must return to the vitamin program.

If you had ear infections as a child and now love milk and
dairy products, you may be allergic to milk. You may be drinking
a lot of it because you are addicted to it or because you are
searching for calcium, but your inefficient intestinal tract cannot
absorb the calcium from the milk.

If you are a young, budding female and your friends find
you irritable (ask them), calcium will be especially helpful for
the next few years. If you are a rapidly growing boy at this age
with muscle cramps and insomnia, you will find that calcium
and magnesium are your friends.

Diet If Your Parents Argue, Fight, Assault Each Other, or Even Hit You

This is very frightening and you must feel the tension in the air. Home is not a comfortable place in which to live, but before you run away or get too sick yourself, there are a few things you might try. Some kids live in homes like this and never bat an eye or lose any sleep over it. They can ignore the mayhem and bedlam and appear very calm and cool. That's tough to do but maybe they are good actors. I'm sure some day all that seething emotion is going to surface and give them some symptoms or at least a rash.

Most children love both of their parents and find it impossible to take sides in the battle. It might do you some good to see if you can diagnose the biochemistry of anger. When two humans are fighting for no good reason, it is probably because they are living in their lower animal brain. It is quite obvious in some adults what alcohol is doing to them; the alcohol deadens some of the nice, human parts of the brain and the falling blood sugar permits only the selfish part of the emotional brain to function. You could try to get them to eat something nourishing when you see them drinking.

Extra magnesium and the B-complex vitamins seem to be the more important nutrients for them to take. See if you can get them to take zinc, 30 to 60 mg, and manganese, 10 to 20 mg daily. We know that the tendency for alcoholism and low blood sugar can run in families, so it would be wise for you to make sure that you never eat sugary things and that you try to nibble on fruit, nuts, seeds, and/or raw vegetables every two to three hours between meals. Vitamin C (1000 to 5000 mg) and the B complex (50 mg of each of the Bs, 100 mcg of B_{12}, and 0.4 mg of folic acid) are good friends, and to help sleep come naturally, use the calcium, 1000 mg, and the magnesium, 750 to 1000 mg, at bedtime.

Diet If You Are Going to Camp, Grandmother's, Boarding School, College, the Military, or Abroad

You might think it a little silly or slightly embarrassing to pull a bag of raw carrots or peanuts from a pocket or purse and begin chewing, but the results can be pleasantly calming at these stressful times. Any stress or change has an effect on the adrenal glands. Cortisol is released to help re-establish homeostasis. If there are no nutritional supplements ingested to satisfy the requirements for the manufacture of these adrenal-gland hormones, a deficiency could be produced and some allergic symptom could appear. The embarrassment of a sneeze, a wheeze, or gas formation would certainly be greater than the private consumption of some good food and some vitamin tablets.

Try to take vitamin C, at least 1000 mg a day; increase the dose if a virus or an allergy is appearing. Take B-complex vitamins at about the 50-mg level daily so your urine is fairly yellow most of the time. Calcium and magnesium work better if taken at bedtime as they have a soporific effect and would help you fall asleep in a strange bed. It is standard to take 1000 mg of calcium, and recently more nutritionists are recommending magnesium at the 750- or 1000-mg level also. It is probably better to take the calcium and magnesium at different times, but it is too much trouble for most of us. Keep meals small and nibble on raw vegetables.

Remember that Adelle Davis thought the bone tumor she developed in her sixties was due to the dreadful dormitory food she ate at age eighteen years.

If you fly, you must remember to exercise in the plane. Stretching and bending in your seat and walking in the aisle is about all that can be done. Learning to cat-nap with your head on your chest is a good trick if you can breathe in this position. Airplane air is very dry; breathing this air and sitting still is very constipating, which is good for airline maintenance but not for your body. Drink fluids; ask for water. I have found that 1000 to 3000 mg of vitamin C daily is the right dose for me while at home with minimal stress. On a two- to four-hour flight I have to eat prunes and dates together with 5 to 10 grams of vitamin C just to keep my bowels working normally. Travelers need B_6, 100 mg twice daily; zinc, 20 to 40 mg; and manganese, 10 to 20 mg a day.

Diet If Your Peer Group Wants You to Take Drugs

This is a tough decision to make. It is almost impossible to get up enough nerve to talk to your parents, your doctor, or your minister, although they all may be ready and willing. They have read all the pamphlets and are anxious to try out the ideas on you. You also know they will counsel you against using anything stronger than a Coke or a sip of wine.

But your friends are right there looking at you and waiting for you to do it. You assume that if you refuse, they will call you chicken and drop you, but you are *really* scared to try. If only they would let you think it over. If you are strong and mature, you might say, "No, thank you, I don't want to wreck my body for future use." Or, "Some other time; that stuff throws off my timing playing the drums."

Most every young person your age seems to feel the need to experiment with drugs. All seem to want to experience an altered state of consciousness. It is such a common thing to do, it almost seems normal. What we parents and doctors worry about is that you might get to *like* the drugged state and then get hooked. Every drug addict was once a cute little baby, as you were.

Many people take drugs because they simply do not feel good and want to feel better. The feeling of boredom and fatigue is especially pronounced at age ten to seventeen years because of the rapid growth. I believe that the ones who are somewhat nervous, or hyper, or restless are the ones more likely to become candidates for illicit drug use. The one who is always jiggling a foot up and down or swinging a leg or a key chain or twisting his or her hair is the one who is more sensitive to the world about him. They are more likely to have mood swings, or get depressed for no reason, or notice feelings of impending doom. They are frequently unable to drop off to sleep at night. Muscle cramps are a reasonably frequent complaint.

See if you can pick out the drug takers in your class by the way they act and how stoned they often are. They are usually irascible and unpredictable. Many of them started to take drugs because they were uncomfortable in the clean state. They frequently perceive the world as close, threatening, overwhelming, coercive, and leaving no room for self-determination, freedom of choice, or autonomy. The boring routine is: get up, do your chores, go to school, come home, do your chores, eat supper, do your homework, go to bed. Some kids thrive on that routine. But it can turn off a lot of young people. The only feeling of power comes in the making of the choice between smoking pot or drinking a beer.

As a little scientific study, do me a favor and write down what these young people are eating and what symptoms they have. The ones with mood swings are usually eating sugar or some food to which they are allergic (milk, soy, corn, wheat, eggs, shellfish, etc.). The restless, twitchy ones are often allergic to milk and are not on any calcium supplement. You might begin a project and help your friends by suggesting that they talk to a doctor about using nutrition so they will not have to rely on drugs. Many of them are suffering from a food allergy, hypoglycemia from sugar or food sensitivities, a calcium or magnesium deficiency, some subtle brain injury, a bad self-image, or a need for the B-complex group of vitamins.

It's too bad we cannot live inside their bodies so we could better perceive what they are perceiving. Many of them simply do not feel good; they find that drugs or alcohol allow them some freedom from pain and discomfort.

Diet If You Are Six to Twelve Years Old and Obviously Getting Fat

It may have sneaked up on you in the last year, because you had a lot of homework to do or the weather was bad and you had to stay home and sit around a lot, but you kept on eating the same amount of food. You might have gotten sick and had to stay quiet for a week or so; you were so enervated it was hard to exercise. Lying in bed will produce a loss of the big leg muscles and these are the main ones that burn up the fat.

Or did you have a tough teacher? Did you feel nervous and tense because a "friend" turned away from you? Were your parents occupied with domestic or financial problems? Did a close, loved relative die?

Did you notice some symptoms that would indicate you have been stressed? Some trouble falling asleep? Crying for no good reason? Poutiness? Irritability? Stomachaches? Nasal stuffiness? Itchy rashes?

Some people only notice weight gain and none of the other symptoms of stress. Some of that problem is genetic. The part of the body that gets hit with the condition is determined by family traits (if your grandmother had eczema, you might acquire the problem when stressed). Most people who gain weight because of stress have parents, aunts, uncles, and/or grandparents who have difficulty keeping their weight under control. That fact doesn't mean it is pointless or worthless for you to aim for the ideal. Don't give up. You just have to be more careful as part of your lifestyle.

Most people your age feel their parents are too strict or have too many rules or are always "on their backs" about chores, cleaning up their rooms, and doing their homework. Your parents' perception may be that you need this prodding. If your schoolwork is okay for your ability, if you have a few friends, and if you can laugh more than you cry, you are doing okay in your life at this time. So, if your life seems to be okay *and* you are gaining weight, then the food you are eating is too heavily loaded with calories, or you are eating something to which you are allergic, or you are not exercising enough. As long as you are growing at least 1¼ inches a year (3 cm), then it suggests your thyroid and growth hormones are sufficient and are not the cause of the weight gain.

In your age group a satisfactory gain is about 5 to 8 pounds a year depending on your muscles and bones and how fast you are growing up. If you are gaining 10 to 12 pounds a year, that is too much; it is tough to get off once it gets onto your frame. Aim to turn these extra pounds from fat to lean muscle. This is best done slowly, not by trying to lose it, but just by gaining less each year. As long as you are growing taller, you should not cheat your body out of essential nutrients. A weight-loss program is too hard to maintain and may give your thyroid gland the wrong messages. If it slows down, you would have even more trouble metabolizing food.

Obviously you must stop the boxed, sugared cereals, the fatty foods (fried chicken and hamburger are one-third fat), pancakes and syrup, potato chips, pie, cake, jam, jellies, sugared and cola drinks—all the things you probably love. Your whole family should be doing this, and it will be easier for you if the goodies are not constantly there as a temptation. Some can stop eating these sugary, fat-filled, and salty foods all at once, but that sudden change is a big stress on most bodies.

Start by just eating a piece of fruit for dessert instead of ice cream or cake. You can tell yourself that the cake will come next week at Joe's party. This diet is not forever; you can cheat occasionally if you eat nutrient-dense foods most of the time. You should notice as time goes by that you crave the goodies less, and when you do eat them, they taste too sweet (or greasy or salty). You might notice that you have more stamina and don't get tired so easily when you give up the sugary stuff.

Your next step is to try to eat five or six small meals a day instead of one or two big ones. This will give you a more even energy supply, so you will *want* to walk, run, or play and hence burn up the calories more efficiently. Remember, the big leg muscles are the main ones that burn up the fat. In a month you will know that you are on the right program because you will feel better and have more energy—and you only gained a half-pound during the time. (Six pounds for the year is your goal.)

If, however, you gained your usual 1 to 2 pounds for the month (12 to 20 pounds for the year), it means you did not eliminate enough goodies, or you are still eating something to which you are allergic, or you did not exercise enough, or you *are* being stressed. You must look around and examine every facet of your life. The extra weight you have will act as its own stressor, because your thin friends will make fun of you and it's just human to eat something for solace when we are the butt of jokes.

You will find that your body will metabolize the food you swallow better if you take some extra B-complex vitamins (a capsule with 50 mg of each of the Bs once or twice a day—note how yellow your urine gets) and chromium (100 mcg a day). This same combination is found in brewer's yeast—2 to 5 teaspoons a day—but most everyone says "Yuk" to brewer's yeast. The tablets are more palatable. Try it for a while for me.

I met a young adolescent the other day who is getting hassled by a tough gang at school. The gang leader is taunting him with words and gestures, but my young friend has maintained his cool exterior. He is nervous inside, but he doesn't want the bully to find out how he really feels. He has some trouble going to sleep at night and his allergies are worse, but the supplements he is taking have kept him from fighting or running. He notices stress but it is not overwhelming or causing symptoms. This is his routine:

• Calcium, 1000 mg a day. He used to take all of this at bedtime because it has a calming effect, but now he finds that calm is what he wants to achieve during the day, so he takes about 300 mg of the calcium in the morning, 300 or so after school, and another 300 to 750 mg at bedtime. He finds it very helpful for muscle aches and growing pains because milk gave him phlegm and earaches.

• Magnesium, 1000 mg a day. He takes this along with the calcium. (Some feel they should not be taken together, as they are absorbed better if ingested at least an hour apart. Not too important.) It increases his tolerance for noise and stress.

• Vitamin B_6 promotes the activity of some of the neurotransmitters in the brain. Zinc, 20 to 40 mg, and manganese, 10 to 20 mg, would be best taken daily. If the human part of the brain is working well, the selfish, surly animal part will not be needed.

Now if my young friend can just get the ugly brute to eat better, maybe his tormentor would feel better and not have to bully people.

Diet If You (Child or Adult) Have Trouble Getting Out of Bed in the Morning

When I was in active practice, parents frequently brought their teenagers into the office to be examined for anemia and mononucleosis. These conscientious parents did not want to feel guilty about prodding and shouting at their children if the problem was some condition that made the children feel tired all the time. Rarely did the examinations reveal anemia or any sickness. We even did skin tests for tuberculosis. At that time we could only suggest a psychiatric approach.

I hearkened back to my own youthful mornings and recalled that although I did get up eventually, it was difficult. I thought that was normal. But when I began to see hundreds of children with a variety of lifestyles, I soon realized that some are owls and some are meadowlarks.

We were taught in medical school that if there were no physical or laboratory explanations for the fatigue, it must be a psychiatric condition; in that case, behavior modification or some sort of psychotherapy was called for. I favored one method: if the child liked school and seemed okay once he or she got there, then the child had to be responsible for not missing the school bus or the first class period. The parent was to awaken the child in plenty of time and have clothes and breakfast laid out so there would be no obstacles. But the adults in the home were to make no comments about time or say "Hurry, you'll be late." It was all up to the child. And if the child was late, he or she had to answer to the teacher. It worked for some.

The behavior modification expert who thought up this self-motivational scheme realized that many children "play games" with their parents, so new approaches must be tried. But if a child does not know the difference between a sock and a piece of toast, the program could be no more than a dirty trick. We believe that many people are not cognitively aware in the A.M. because their blood sugar is low. Children may be the most likely victims because the child's brain has two to three times the energy needs of the adult brain. The food from yesterday may all be burned or stored and there is no glucose available for the continuous energy needs of the neocortex. Without the neocortex the child might just eat his sock and put his toast on his foot. That busy part of the brain has a conscience; it has stored memory for the date, the child's name, his address, and almost everything that he has perceived since the neocortex began to operate. If it does not operate well, the owner might act just like a hibernating animal aroused in January.

The trick, then, is to eat something at bedtime that will release its energy so slowly over the eight to twelve sleeping hours that some energy will still be available for the rousing hour. Some do better if they eat nothing between supper and bedtime, so that the blood sugar just slowly slips away until breakfast. Typically, the people who have trouble getting up are the ones who eat ice cream or a sugary snack or even fruit while they watch TV before retiring. What determines the status of the brain at 7 A.M. is usually not the hour we went to bed, but the biochemistry of the bloodstream. Your bedtime snack should be a handful of nuts, a piece of cheese, an egg, or a bit of leftover meat—something that will break down slowly through the night. Try it and let me know.

7

Diets for
Stressful
Occupations

Different jobs put different stresses on people.
And sometimes the stress can be devastating. It is no surprise
to me to learn that one of the highest rates of miscarriages and
inability to conceive is found among operating room nurses. The
chief surgeon has a stressful job, because he or she is responsible
for the life of the patient on the operating table. The surgeon
must have the proper scalpel, the perfect light, the right-colored
drapes. If something does not go well, the operating room nurse
is sometimes the first one to feel the surgeon's wrath.

Another work-related stress—and much underestimated—
occurs on the retirement of a hard-working, trusted employee
after thirty good and devoted years with the mother company.
The ceremony is over, he or she gets the gold watch, and that's
it. *No one needs me anymore.* That's a stress which starts a
downhill slide for many. We all need to feel that we are decent,
worthwhile, and useful individuals.

There have been many studies of why some people lead

long and happy lives. They all say the secret is this: The elderly person always wanted to get up and go to work in the morning. Nutrition plays a role in this. If you eat the wrong foods you may not even know your name in the morning, much less what you are supposed to be doing. ("Is it Sunday or Monday? I'll get the paper from the porch. If it's heavy, it's Sunday and I won't have to go to work.")

Recognizing that our jobs involve stress is the first step. You may have to live with that stress, but you don't have to be undermined by it. Find yourself in the occupational profiles that follow. Follow the Dr. Smith's Diet that is right for your physiology (phases One through Six), and add the nutritional and lifestyle supports suggested for people in your particular occupation. Your program for job survival and job success must satisfy not merely your physiological requirements, but your emotional needs as well.

Diet for Drivers

(Cab driver, limousine driver, truck driver, pilot, locomotive engineer.)

People who drive or pilot for a living are in danger of getting heavy because they sit on their buns all the time they are working. They are so intent on getting where they're going that they give no thought to exercise. Their supervisors or bosses should make some kind of rule about exercise. (Every hour, the driver must get out of the cab or truck and walk, or do push-ups, or jog a bit on a side road. Something!)

A recent study indicated that about 75 percent of the pilots of one airline company had the hypoglycemic tendency. I do worry when I see the flight attendant taking a coke or coffee with sugar into the cockpit. I figure if we land in twenty to forty minutes we will be okay, but after that the pilot may not be operating on all the necessary cortical neurons he needs to land this big hunk of metal, screws, and wires.

My wife and I found that we did much better on a long trip if we took the children along, even though they were a wild and crazy bunch in the car. Their activity level forced us to stop the car and let them (and us) explode outside for just five minutes. We *all* felt better after walking or running along the road shoulder or playing tag at a rest stop. We also did better if we ate raw vegetables, fruit, seeds, and nuts, and drank only water. Never—driver or passenger—drink a cola drink or have cookies while in a moving car.

Not all drivers/pilots were hyper kids, so maybe you are not one of those with a tendency to low blood sugar that will make you fall asleep, get angry, or get fat if you eat quick carbos. Many people will drift off to sleep when hypnotized by the boring road. Years ago I used to take a thermos of black coffee along for any trip over forty miles. It was the worst thing I could have done, as I later realized, because I am allergic and can become addicted to caffeine. This dawned on me after I read an article about hyperactive children who were sedated in the classroom if they drank coffee. Stimulants calm them. I made the connection: I am a somewhat hyperactive, restless type, and the reason I slept well at night was that I drank coffee at bedtime!

I decided to give up coffee altogether. There were a few withdrawal headaches but no big deal. I stopped eating cookies daily and began to nibble on raw vegetables, fruit, seeds, and nuts. I am 70 percent better, but I still do better if my wife rides in the car with me.

Many truck drivers, I have heard, take amphetamines to stay awake for those long trips across country. If you were a hyper kid, these stimulants (Dexedrine, Ritalin, Cylert, and coffee and tea) might be still having a calming effect on you to the point of somnolence. Try the seeds, nuts, fruits, and vegetables, and a strong B complex (50 mg of a lot of the Bs: B_1, 50 mg; B_2, 50 mg; B_3, 50 mg; B_6, 50 mg; B_{12}, 50 mcg). For many, this has a stimulating effect (due to histamine release). If it really gooses you, it suggests you are low in calcium. Therefore, at the end of the run, if you want to take a nap or relax and sleep, ingest 500 to 1000 mg of calcium and about the same amount of magnesium. You should enjoy one to six hours of sleep and be able to awaken without a drugged feeling.

People who sit a lot tend to become constipated; hard, dry stools are the lot of many drivers. It surprises and saddens me that so many people are unaware that small, firm stools are not normal and are frequently the result of a sedentary life and low-fiber, low-roughage foods. Dairy products are the number one culprit, but sugar and white flour products are close seconds. Bran from grains, and fiber in prunes, dates, and figs should soften the toughest stools by holding moisture in the fecal mass. It might even make a lethargic, enervated driver more likely to exercise because he or she must find a toilet or a secluded spot to dump the rectal load. At the least, you should have a soft bulky movement once a day. Hemorrhoids don't come from sitting on cold cement or the hard seats of a truck; they come from hard bowel movements that sit on the pelvic veins and cause the circulation to back up.

Diet for Those Who Must Deal with People Who Are Sometimes Surly, Disinterested, Negative, Demanding, Stupid, Impossible, Drunk, Noncompliant, Argumentative (but You Cannot Say It to Their Faces)

(Teacher, housewife, househusband, professor, doctor, school bus driver, waiter, waitress, nurse, flight attendant, parking lot attendant, priest, sister, minister, salesperson, city or county administrator or commissioner, senator, congressional representative, supervisor, sergeant, captain, agent.)

These people *really* need a good support system in the profession, the family, the religious hierarchy, the political structure, or the company. These are the ones who should have a good self-image before they even decide to take up any of these professions. Maybe a psychometric study (Minnesota Multiphasic) or a projective test (Rorschach) would be helpful for the eighteen-year-old who is interested in taking up one of these careers.

Can you remember your folks saying nice things about you? Were they supportive of you in school, and did they take your side when there were differences of opinion? Or did you feel put down by your peers, parents, and teachers? Did you tend to feel stupid? Were you told you did not work up to your potential? Did you wet the bed, have allergies, cry easily, or feel ticklish? These things suggest you are sensitive. Under pressure you might blow your cool too easily, or make stupid decisions, or get a psychosomatic illness. Hiatal hernia is a common disorder among flight attendants. So are constipation and hemorrhoids. Just when you have a call of nature, they announce that the plane is about to take off or land. Buckle up. Too bad; you're stuck. The longer the bowel movement stays in there, the harder it is to push it out. And you get dehydrated because the air in those planes is very dry.

But if you are reading this after you have started working in one of these jobs or professions, you can still reorganize your life and make your work a rewarding challenge instead of a screaming stress. Calcium and magnesium are the backbone of self-control. They allow you to say "It's okay" when someone is shouting, "You are stupid" or "I'm going to sue you!" or "You made a mistake, buster."

I had plenty of that in a busy four-man pediatric office. I thought my bouts of depression, crying, and headaches came from being overconscientious or from bottling up my hostility. Demanding patients expected me to be available, cheerful, supportive, intelligent, and gentle with their children. I had read in psychiatric texts that unresolved aggression might back up on the victim or would appear as a psychosomatic headache, or ulcers, or hypertension. But on a better diet—no cookies and no coffee—my headaches were gone. Apparently I did not have unresolved hatred for anyone, and I was still the same nice, conscientious doctor. It helped to have a supportive wife who was always reliable and a model mother. I also found release in playing the clarinet and acting in plays.

If you find that you have any psychosomatic symptoms— obesity, headaches, eczema, asthma, colitis, gas, insomnia, hay fever, depression, crying spells, nervousness, fatigue, tightness in the neck and back, and if you are getting sarcastic with the clients and becoming just as obnoxious as the customers, you might try the following before you take up Valium, booze, antacids, or psychotherapy:

Change your diet. Get off the coffee and cola drinks. Stay away from sugar, salt, greasy foods, and white flour. Nibble on seeds, nuts, raw vegetables, and fruit—small amounts frequently. Stop any food you love or are eating daily; it could be an allergen. Follow the Dr. Smith's Low-Stress Weight Control Diet on page 53.

Flight attendants tell me that they can handle the stresses of nervous passengers, hyperactive children, vomiting overeaters, loud drunks, and amorous pinchers, by staying away from the food served on the flights. (The toughest passenger is the one who has been stressed from the last flight and takes it out on the innocent attendant of the present flight.) The attendants believe the problem with the food is the additives and preservatives needed to keep it "fresh." They tell me that they feel better if they nibble on small amounts of raw vegetables, fruits, nuts, and seeds which they bring from home. Apparently we humans can handle stress if we keep the blood sugar at a moderate and even level.

These supplements should provide extra help: vitamin C, 1000 to 5000 mg daily, depending upon the bowel activity; vitamin B_3 (niacinamide), 500 to 2000 mg a day, if you (or your friends and lovers) notice that you are touchy, withdrawn, or on the edge of paranoia; vitamin B_6, 50 to 200 mg a day, to help your brain and your adrenals. You would know that it is necessary if you cannot remember your dreams.

Diet If You Do Nit-Picking, Boring Work

(Typist, housewife, househusband, secretary (sometimes), barber, baker, assembly-line worker, computer operator, dishwasher, clerk, television studio crew, copy editor, accountant, baggage handler, stock boy, letter carrier, bricklayer, candlestick maker.)

I would think these jobs must be the pits. They represent many working situations wherein autonomy can appear to be lost. *Here is a job; do it.* There is very little creativity, and little chance to use the imagination. In most of these jobs, human interaction is minimal. We are, after all, human beings, and human contacts are necessary for meaningful life. Motherhood can be rewarding, but being a houseperson is usually dullsville.

If you have a job like this, I would hope that you also have a good, positive relationship with another human being.

I talked with a doctor who is responsible for the health of all the men who work at the local brewery. He says most all of them who have worked there for more than ten years really look sick—soft, doughy, pale skin, circles under their eyes, and enlarged livers. Most are overweight, tired, and bored. Same routine every day. Sounds like a dull, lackluster, death-on-the-rockpile existence. To liven things up, the union negotiated as a side benefit that each worker would be given a six-pack every day. You probably went to work at the beer factory because you liked beer, and when you got six cans a day *free* you would feel you were set for life. Reach for the *gusto!* Then gradually you got bored, and because there were no great challenges on the job, you found it helped to have one beer, just one, for lunch. Then it was two, and after a year or so there was nothing left of the six-pack to bring home at the end of the day. Who cares anyway? You get your supper down, watch some television, and fall asleep in the chair until bedtime. A perceptive boss or supervisor would notice your loss of efficiency on the job and blow the whistle on you or send you to the company doctor.

Are you having any symptoms? Headaches, weight gain, stomachaches, hating to get out of bed in the morning after eight hours' sleep? If you are, then the job is affecting you. Boredom could be a stress. If you have no symptoms, then maybe the job is just right for you, or your goals and expectations are equal to the reality, or your private life is really fulfilling. But you do have choices. Could you possibly make your hobby into your job or start a cottage industry? You have all your life to live. If you feel trapped, you could take an extension course, nose around, find something a little more exciting.

If you are restless and dissatisfied, you are experiencing loss of autonomy and it's going to wear you down. If you think you are too tired and fat to make an effort to move into another, more satisfying line, then try the diet and the supplements.

Diet If You Are Dealing with People under Stress

(Police officer, surgeon, mortician, lawyer, telephone operator, psychiatrist, psychologist, counselor, reporter, pediatrician, judge, minister, welfare worker, probation officer, emergency room doctor or nurse.)

You probably went into this type of work because you are somewhat altruistic and wanted to help people. You find that many of your clients turn on you just when you think you are doing the most good. It's draining.

Two psychiatrists were leaving their offices at 5 P.M. The younger one, who appeared disheveled and worn, said to his colleague, "You look so fresh and unruffled. How can you listen to all those problems of sick people all day and not get washed out?"

The older one's measured response: "Who listens?"

Many people seem to have the ability to be concerned and responsive without getting so involved that it throws their own bodies and feelings off kilter. They are able to remain at the edge of things. Many like the challenge of a job where they have to be always ready for a sudden emergency. But a high-quality diet and an exercise program are requirements to be able to meet the demands placed on anyone desiring these lines of work.

A study of the Portland Police Bureau was conducted by the University of Washington. It was designed to determine the sources of stress for the officers and to devise techniques for dealing effectively with the stress. A large source of stress, the study found, was the frequent change of work hours. In its efforts to be fair, the administration had everyone changing from nights to days, from days to swing shift, and from swing shift to nights— *every ten days.* The officers got tired and grouchy because their biological clocks were screwed up; just when they were getting used to one shift, they would have to change. Under the new plan, each member of the force decides what shift to take and he or she stays with it for years or until retirement. Much less stress. (Those on the night shift do better if they take some extra vitamin A, 20,000 to 30,000 units; it helps control night blindness.)

Those of us who deal with other human beings should never have to deal with anything but the neocortex, the human, humane part of the nervous system. Psychotherapy is worthless at the spinal-cord level—for the therapist as well as the patient. Psychiatrists, counselors, psychologists, and therapists should have bowls of nuts, seeds, fruit, and raw veggies in their waiting rooms and on the table next to the consultation couch. Many hotel registration desks have a basket of fruit within reach; a tired and hungry traveler may forget to complain if offered something to eat. It takes about twenty minutes for the fruit to elevate the blood sugar to the point where the surly guest's mood changes from paranoia ("What kind of service is this!") to friendliness

("Hey, you folks are okay!"). Saying "Have a good day" to a snake is dumb.

I would not mind paying my phone bill if the operators would just be cheerful while I'm reaching out to "touch someone." Could the switchboard supervisors put out some wholesome nibbly-type food for the operators so they would be able to handle the less-than-perfect customers?

Many workers in this general category complain that they haven't the time to get a "decent meal." By a "decent meal" do they mean a steak, french-fried potatoes, and overcooked, dead vegetables? Better not even to go into the places that serve this food. "But I can't fix lunch before I leave home. I don't have time." (Read the section about getting out of bed in the morning.)

I have little trouble getting a cheap, filling lunch in the standard supermarket. I make a quick dash to the produce section; almost all the vegetables there can and should be eaten raw. (Don't eat uncooked corn, potatoes, eggplant, beans, or anything that has a waxy coat. Humans don't have the proper enzymes to digest them.) Turnips, parsnips, and rutabagas are just as tasty as the carrots, beets, and celery. (I once consumed a whole turnip before I got to the checkout stand.) A small brick of low-fat, low-salt, *unprocessed* cheese (processed often has aluminum in it) would supply some protein and calcium. Have a piece of fruit for dessert and maybe a bag of unsalted nuts or seeds. A can of low-sugar fruit drink can be swallowed about an hour after the rest has been eaten. Take some raisins or other dried fruit for a midafternoon snack. You can get a big meal for just two or three dollars.

Morticians have to be open, friendly, caring, and full of human kindness. It is their job to try to comfort newly grieving strangers. That's hard to do when you don't feel good. Morticians, especially, need a good self-image, much patience, and great strength. They need a sense of humor (but there are times when jokes are in bad taste).

Being human and supportive, and getting paid for it, must be the best kind of job in the world. This is why there are so many young people clamoring to go into medicine. But if the doctor notices that too many of his patients are becoming clients of the mortician, the result is stress. One little mistied suture could show the world he should be lecturing, not operating. And one missed breakfast could prevent his brain from telling his surgeon's hands what to do when all that blood wells up into the surgical wound.

Surgeons should eat before performing surgery and afterward also. It should not be just coffee and a doughnut. They need food that lasts, so when they finally go home and the garbage needs to be taken out, they can do it and think it is fun.

It is possible for doctors to miss diagnoses because a bad headache keeps them from concentrating on what a parent is telling them about a sick child. Patients have switched to other pediatricians because they happened to call me before supper. What they contacted then was my animal brain; they got a mean, surly little kid for a doctor.

I've been in the newsrooms of large and small newspapers around the country. I've seen the cigarette smoke layered across the desks and undulating under the fluorescent (not full-spectrum) lights.[1] I've seen the huge coffee maker emptied every two hours. In general, the people who work there seem pale and nervous, with dark circles under their eyes; many are jiggling a foot up and down or swinging a leg. Do they smoke, drink coffee, and booze because they are living the movie image? Is it really a stress to live daily with stress on all sides? Or does it seem stressful to them because of what they are eating and drinking? I don't think I've met a newspaperperson who did not

1. These help compensate for the stress of working under fluorescent lights: calcium, magnesium, B_2 (50 mg), and vitamin A (20,000 to 30,000 units).

have some physical or psychosomatic complaint. No time to eat? Nonsense! They could write exciting stories *and* take care of their health at the same time.

I would expect a judge to have mixed feelings about his or her job. Judges are bright, often brilliant, but the intellectual challenges are not always present to keep them from dozing off. Judges must have filed away in their brains hundreds of rulings and procedures ready to use for the case they are trying. One goof and the whole world will know, because the court stenographer is taking everything down. A judge *has* to keep the blood sugar at an optimal level. Much courtroom business is routine and dull, but if the judge's mind is wandering when something needs his or her swift attention, it could be very embarrassing.

I was a witness at a trial and observed how one judge solved his blood sugar problem. He peeled and ate an orange at about 11 A.M., midway through the morning. Many judges jog in the morning, play racquetball at noon, and garden in the late afternoon. Many judges are learning about the crime-inducing effects of a nutrient-poor diet. A few are experiencing the salutary effects of good food and exercise and are now promoting this as part of the probation requirements. Recidivism is reduced.

Probation officers and welfare workers have a high burnout rate because they give so much and get back so little. If they would encourage the use of good food and exercise, for themselves and their clients, they would see a higher percentage of their charges climbing up from this bottom rung of the social ladder and they, in turn, would feel better about their work. They deal with people who are considered losers, and losers often have low self-esteem. This can be contagious.

If you social workers and probation officers could just direct these people into better eating habits and get them off their dope and cigarettes, if you could show them that they do have some autonomy, *your* job would take on some real meaning. The control you have over their lives can lead them to a good feeling of energy and cheerfulness. If they are better, you will think your job is rewarding.

Diet for Those Whose Jobs Require Sudden Bursts of Energy

(Ambulance driver, medic, helicopter pilot on call, obstetrician, athlete, fireman, actor, TV or radio performer, ballet dancer, musician, farmer, neurosurgeon, cardiac surgeon, student, fisherman, SWAT team member, air traffic controller.)

Some of these workers and professionals are interrupted in their sleep. In general, they have a bad schedule and they have very little control over it. Firemen are a prime example. It may be that the fireman has the most stressful and dangerous job of all. He can be bored to death one minute and then be catapulted the next into a five-alarm burning chemical plant, unable to see for the smoke, freezing then burning, choking on the fumes, saving lives and getting little acclaim because no one could see what he did, and all because some sociopath who probably doesn't eat right threw a match into a warehouse.

The body does not like sudden changes: hot/cold, quiet/active, sleepy/wakeful, hungry/full. All sorts of chemical and nervous system events take place to restore homeostasis. The adrenal glands are the key to this reaction. If stressful events are repeated with little chance for these glands to recover from the last episode, something gives. The victim becomes allergic, obese, gets sick in some psychosomatic way. If this condition deteriorates further into a fear of the job or depression or even craziness, it is called "burn-out."

I would expect the people in this category to be more likely than all the rest to experience symptoms earlier in their lives. Obstetricians tend to limit or discontinue their practice after twenty years because they become aware that deliveries seem to come at night, just nine months after fertilization. Getting up at night, even for a birth, is a real stress, especially if one has been working hard all day in a busy office. At least firemen and most other workers have shifts and usually know when they are off duty.

Medicine is an unrelenting and tough master. The rewards of prestige and good pay almost balance the rotten hours. This has to be the motivation of the neurosurgeon. Imagine a six- to twelve-hour operation digging about in someone's brain. If I were the one on the table, I would hope my surgeon had had a good night's sleep and maybe a steak for breakfast. He'd never get past the first layer if he had eaten only frosted flakes and orange juice. With that stuff for breakfast, his neocortex would be nourished for not more than twenty minutes. "Sorry," it might apologize, "I guess there's nothing more I can do on just sugar."

Or how about the cardiac bypass surgeon who has done three big ones during the day and has to perform another at 1 A.M.? If he keeps up this pace, he might be the next candidate for heart failure. Both these surgical specialties, as well as cancer surgery, have a high mortality rate. That's also a stress when you labor conscientiously all night and the patient dies!

All these folks need a really good diet (Broughton's "foods to remember"), and they must carry about with them some goodies to provide long-term energy. Vitamin C sufficient to soften the stools is great for people with stress, but I would prefer one good, soft bowel movement a day rather than three if I were a surgeon. Diarrhea does wreck one's attention span. Regulate the dose so your stools are on the edge of sloppiness.

Athletes are fooling themselves if they still eat steak, eggs, a quart of milk, and three potatoes before the big game. All that protein is a waste of food. They need long-acting carbohydrates (*see* food lists, Chapter 5) which are stored as glycogen in the muscles for future use. Quick-acting sugar—as in soft drinks, Gatorade, and the other nonfoods—would be good if one were to run the 10-yard dash; that's about all they are good for.

Participants in contact sports will have fewer bruises, and

the ones they do get will heal faster, if they take at least 1000 mg of vitamin C two or three times during a game. The bio-flavonoids, 50 to 100 mg, along with the C, help the integrity of the capillaries. Zinc, 30 to 60 mg, and vitamin A, 20,000 units, would help heal skin chafed from friction with the equipment and the playing surface and would quiet contact rashes from the straps, rubber pads, and belts. If protein is helpful, vitamin B complex is needed, especially B_6 (100 to 200 mg a day). Calcium, 1000 mg, and magnesium, 750 mg or more would best be taken at bedtime to soothe the aching muscles and promote drug-free sleep. Milk creates phlegm in many, so runners who need to breathe well might be wise to stay away from it for a few days before an event. Vitamin E, 400 to 1200 units, is a scavenger and definitely helps endurance in any situation where oxygen needs are increased.

Actors and TV and radio performers frequently have a childhood history of hyperactivity, talkativeness, allergies, and put-downs. They seem to have a strong need to win and are devastated if they do not get rave reviews. They are often shy but they love people and need feedback. They get so nervous because of these traits that they frequently fall victim to drugs and alcohol. (Blue- and green-eyed ones seem especially prone to all the above.) They have to keep their blood sugar up all the time, because when it drops and someone offers them a drink as a "pick-me-up" they may be off on a five-day binge. Alcoholics usually are thin, but the same biochemical mechanism is operating for the obese. Stress hits, blood sugar falls, pass the chocolate or the booze.

Theater owners, play and movie producers, and managers of TV stations should always provide as part of the working conditions the "foods to remember": nuts, seeds, fruits, and vegetables. If these are around, someone will eat them. (I wonder if someday there will be a class-action suit alleging that because the employer did not provide these good foods, an employee developed alcoholism or obesity.)

People whose work subjects them to sudden, unpredictable demands function best on a no-sugar, complex carbohydrate diet with five meals a day and frequent, small feedings of protein. If the sweets and candy bars are around, these people will eat them. Somehow their personalities push them into a stressful type of work that requires attention, sudden bursts of speed and energy, and a competitive spirit. The good diet plus calcium, magnesium, vitamin C, and the B complex should help them stay away from drugs and booze. They must learn to recognize what stress is doing to them and counteract this with diet, exercise, and supplements. Otherwise they are at risk of falling into the drug-drink pit.

Diet if You Work in an Environment with Extremes of Temperature, or You Are Exposed to Toxins, Chemicals, or Heavy Metals

(Plumber, welder, miner, carpenter, electrician, automotive worker, mechanic, battery maker, chemical worker, painter, printer, pathologist, anesthesiologist, perfume factory worker, asbestos worker, petroleum industry worker, cigarette smoker.)

These people are breathing, touching, and swallowing chemicals on the job, and the body has to detoxify the chemicals and get rid of them via the exhaled air, the feces, the urine, and the sweat.

Taking vitamin C, 5000 to 10,000 mg a day, or enough to just soften the bowel movements a bit, would be wise. Vitamin C is especially important for those exposed to high temperatures; it is an effective antidote for prickly heat. Vitamin C also promotes the detoxification of chemicals and heavy metals.

Zinc, 60 to 90 mg, helps rid the body of some of the heavy metals. Manganese, 10 to 20 mg, should be taken with zinc, 30 to 60 mg. Calcium, 1000 mg, and magnesium, 1000 mg, are standard doses for everyone to keep the heavy metals from getting inside.

Vitamin A and its precursor, beta-carotene (found in carrots and the yellow and green vegetables), have proven useful in protecting the lungs of smokers from cancer. These vitamins are well known for aiding the mucous membranes.

Selenium is known to be valuable for humans exposed to chemical poisons; 100 to 150 mcg a day would be about right. Vitamin E is a well-known detoxifier. As the pollutants and smog increase, so should the dose. The minimum dose would be 400 units a day; 1200 to 2000 would be standard for those heavily exposed to noxious chemicals.

8

Nutrition for "No-Choice" Situations

In the spring of 1983 I was asked to speak before a group of osteopathic physicians. They seemed bright, cheerful, and anxious to learn. So for a good hour I gave them the cream of what I've learned over the years. On the same program, a Dr. Gordon H. Deckert of Oklahoma City, Oklahoma, gave them a lively, thought-provoking talk. He is a psychiatrist who has made a special study of the way facial clues reveal emotional states. His message to these doctors was that they could enhance their therapeutic abilities by learning to perceive depression on a patient's face. Treatment aimed at alleviating that problem can be started sooner if the doctor doesn't keep waiting for the patient to say, "I'm depressed."

But it was another aspect of Dr. Deckert's talk that set me thinking. This was his delineation of the effects on us of a perceived loss of autonomy. When people feel that they have few or no choices in their lives, that is a serious stress. And it is very common for people to be under this stress.

149

Dr. Deckert performed a little skit at the meeting, using his wife to illustrate how stress affects people and how to recognize it. He threw this curve at her: "Hello, dear, I've just been elected to the presidency of the Oklahoma Psychiatric Society!"

Mrs. Deckert stood quietly, her head bowed. It looked as if the news was about the worst thing she could have heard. She sighed, "Oh."

Her husband showed the audience what a clever diagnostician he was by remarking, "I see you are depressed."

"Yes." She took a deep breath and exhaled slowly and forcefully. "You're gone so much now with meetings and patients. I thought we were going to have a better year." Sigh.

Dr. Deckert turned to the audience. "This scenario is too close for comfort." It was a forceful demonstration: a woman feeling herself even more stuck at home. No way out.

Watching it, I began to consider the implications it might have for all kinds of symptoms. In particular, I wondered if women may be more susceptible to weight gain (one study indicates 75 percent of younger women believe they are overweight)[1] because they perceive, somehow, that they have lost some autonomy. They are stuck with the hormones that enlarge their hips and breasts and put a layer of fat under their skin. They were used to living inside a relatively free-flowing, easy-to-move body until the age of ten or eleven years. And now, with "too much" fat and not enough muscle, they cannot keep up with their male peers. Women know that *they* have to have the menstrual periods. *They* have to have the babies. *They* have to be so careful of the male's fragile ego. *They* have to be satisfied with two-thirds pay for equal work. *They* get the blame if the children have psychological problems. (Do women go to work

1. In the February 1984 issue (pages 198 to 201), *Glamour* magazine reported the results of a reader survey done in 1983. While 75 percent of the respondents perceived themselves as needing to lose weight, only 25 percent were above normal height/weight standards.

so they won't have to feel guilty about the child's bad behavior? "The baby sitter caused it.") Some of these situations are getting better, but these stresses for women will always be there. And they turn on the issue of autonomy.

A parallel explanation fits the difficulty that many women have when they try to get back to their prepregnancy weight after their first child. They may have a perception that the extra weight (20 to 30 pounds) is really a part of themselves. With the baby comes responsibility. The future is all decided: eighteen years of child-rearing and the PTA. There seem to be no choices.

The loss of control seems to be a motivating force in increasing incidence of anorexia nervosa and bulimia in young women. They perceive that life has no options for them; they are being manipulated by parents, school, life, hormones, and the only way they have to express their independence (or control) is by not eating (or eating and purging or vomiting). They lose weight, their periods stop (they stop being female), and friends and family cluster about urging them to eat. This passive-aggressive act soon leads to vitamin and mineral deficiencies severe enough to shut down the biochemistry of the body and bring on a secondary anorexia. Psychogenic anorexia leads to nutritional anorexia; the disease causes the perpetuation of the disease.

When I started my survey of cab drivers I thought the problems would be fairly obvious. The older drivers were generally glum and monosyllabic. Most of them smoked, drank cola drinks or coffee with sugar, and just sat there waiting for a fare. I asked one, "How do you react when your passenger is late to the airport, but it's the rush-hour traffic and not your fault, and the fare is saying, 'I'm late, you S.O.B. You made me late!'?"

"I just let it run in one ear and out the other," he answered. I wish more of us could handle stress like that.

Then I got a hint of an unexpected stress. A cab driver in

Cincinnati and another in Philadelphia both told me of their preference for cab driving over limousine driving.

"Really? I thought the limo would be the perfect job: dressy uniform, good tips, great car, and some prestige."

"No," they seemed sure. "Because when we get to the destination, the fare says, 'Wait.' It may be fifteen minutes or four hours. You wait."

"Oh," I thought; it must be that they are all so hyper, they need to keep moving. But now I realize that part of the dissatisfaction in just sitting and waiting is the sense of having no control over the situation. It represents a loss of autonomy. I might read a book or take a nap or write letters, but cab drivers go into that business because they need to move; reading and writing are not "their things."

A recent conversation with a Chicago driver revealed even another stress—at least for him. He hated limousine driving because he wasn't able to talk to the fare. He also admitted to being on Antabuse for his alcoholism. Alcoholics are great talkers. They also have hypoglycemia. And this cab driver—predictably—was overweight.

No-choice situations come to us all at one time or another. I'm referring to the really tough things that life can hand us, seemingly by chance, as if it were our turn to get stomped on. The death of a spouse, a divorce, foreclosure on the mortgage— such events are a powerful challenge to our physical and emotional balance. To survive these things, to be able to handle the stress, we need to follow an appropriate diet. But what happens so often is that the frustration and the need to alleviate the emotional pain of these events tip the victims into eating patterns that lead to obesity.

When something devastating happens to you, you are entitled to notice symptoms of stress. Indeed, if you do *not* notice depression, anxiety, weight gain, or desire to drink or eat or smoke, then either you are unfeeling or a schizoid personality type, or you really *can* handle stress.

Let us now look at some of the events that are generally accepted to be destructive stressors and see how diet can be our friend in helping us survive these unhappy episodes.

The death of a spouse certainly satisfies the criteria that define a stressor. There is complete loss of autonomy. One is stuck.

A psychosomatic illness appears because a problem was not dealt with at the conscious level. The psychosomatic symptoms may fulfill a purpose or provide a secondary gain. It may be a way for a "trapped person" to express some autonomy or control over the environment. Psychiatric intervention to explore guilt, depression, resentment, and anger seem appropriate.

Despite the psychiatric implications of the depression that follows the loss of a loved one, we must all be cognizant of the biochemical changes that accompany any severe stressful event. Some loved one must make sure that vitamin C is taken in larger than usual doses; perhaps 2000 to 10,000 mg a day. A B-complex capsule should be taken daily, one with 50 to 100 mg of each of the Bs in it, plus 100 mcg of B_{12} and 0.4 mg of folic acid. A grieving person would be likely to have insomnia because of low calcium. Calcium should be tried at bedtime in preference to pills; it is cheap and safe and more likely to be the missing element. (I doubt that the patient would have a Valium deficiency.) Magnesium usually is taken along with the calcium, and the experts now feel it should be taken in about the same amounts as the calcium. People who have been grieving for too long a period of time often will become socially responsive and more cheerful, renew their sense of humor, and even re-establish a clear, pink complexion after a few weeks on niacinamide, 1000 to 3000 mg daily. There is no choice. There is no bringing the loved one back.

Guilt enters into the picture. Who wouldn't feel, "If I had just called the doctor sooner!" Then comes anger at the loss: "I put all that love and time and effort into you, and you left me." And then finally comes acceptance. Life does go on. It can take six months to a year to get over the grief.

Who thinks about food and vitamins at a time like this? Who cares? Most stop eating at their usual level: "Cooking is pointless; there's no one here to eat. I'm not hungry anyway." The depression can be so overwhelming and create such a shutdown of energy flow that the victim could easily gain weight because he or she is just sitting, staring out into space (or at the tube). Often a depressed person will cut back on food ingestion so that a balance between intake and outgo develops and weight stays the same. But if the person does not eat enough high-quality, nutrient-dense foods to supply minerals and the B-complex vitamins, a biochemical stress occurs that reinforces the emotional stress. If one quietly sits and eats little, the thyroid tends to cut back; small amounts of food will tend to be stored and not burned.

Severe stress will make the blood sugar drop and force the adrenals to secrete cortisol and adrenalin. If these glands are not nourished, any number of psychosomatic diseases will surface. Allergies, colitis, infections, backache, skin rashes, fatigue, may all occur sequentially, related to the loss. Obesity is a common result.

Divorce, separation, jail term, severe or chronic illness in a family member, job loss, unwanted pregnancy, financial reverses, change of work, rape, or death of an intimate friend, foreclosure of a mortgage, and loss of home through fire or storm are all stresses that could really crush a family that is only barely holding itself together.

In the first situation—divorce—at least one member of the diad must show anger sufficient to hire a lawyer and take steps to get the spouse out of his or her life. The initiator (plaintiff) of the divorce or separation may have no symptoms to suggest the stress that is going on, but the defendant would feel the anger, the anxiety, and the loss of autonomy. "What did I do that deserves all this hostility? I knew we had problems, but they couldn't have been as bad as all that."

My wife and I had similar feelings when our house was

burglarized. "What had we done to deserve that? What did we do to you that you would do this to us?"

If you are in any one of these situations and you *do not* notice any anxiety, weight gain, or other symptoms, you are unusual. But your physiology might be compromised to the extent that twenty years from now you may get some complaint from some part of your body. These disruptions are stressful and you would be prudent to eat properly and take some supplements of C, B complex, and calcium, and talk to a good listening friend or a psychotherapist. (Sometimes it is more valuable to pay an objective listener for an opinion.)

Most of us try to get involved with another person or a group that we can call on for support. We all need this kind of sharing, and if our needs are not fulfilled, we back out and find another "family." A family provides—ideally—nurturing, attention, and recognition. These qualities are more or less expected from anyone with whom we live. And we give them the same things. Quid pro quo. In a family we should be able to enjoy both some privacy and some intimacy. Everyone in a relationship should be able to feel that he or she has a sense of personal power (autonomy). There should be choices.

I suppose the ideal would be to ask our spouse or lover each day, "How are you doing? Are you satisfied with our relationship? Are you having fun? Do you feel you have enough autonomy?" If your sharer doesn't understand that word, or what you are driving at, ask, "Do you feel free? Do you see light at the end of the tunnel? Do you like to get out of bed in the morning?"

We should also try to notice if our spouse or lover has any psychosomatic symptoms. *Those* might be clues that he or she is experiencing stress. Usually it is not a conscious stress; if it were conscious, he or she would say it loud and clear. If someone you are connected with (married to, living with, dear friend of) has periodic attacks of colitis, weight gain, asthma, or tics and twitches, consider whether you might be the cause of the stress response. Does the other experience *you* as a stress? I know my wife felt that my behavior and idiosyncrasies were worse just before her periods. She knew the vitamins and minerals were helpful, but she also felt that if I would not stress her, she would not need the supplements. The mind affects the body, and one mind can affect another mind. We are all connected.

But remember, a poor or inappropriate diet will allow the neocortex to notice stress where none was present. This is partly why Christmas and vacations can be a stress, for individuals as well as for families. Every Christmas the local TV talk shows invite a psychologist to talk about holiday depression. The theory behind the depression is that the season is not as it was when you were four years old. Your mother is now worn and senile, your dad is gone from overwork, and life is not simple anymore. You feel gypped and cheated and you have every right to feel depressed.

Although all of the above is true, and the promise of the season may turn out to be a hollow, commercial sham, the real cause for your dip in mood may be that you are drinking booze and eating yule cake. That fruitcake you got last year is not to be eaten; it is to be sent to a friend, or better yet, to a relative, *this* year; he or she will send it on. Don't eat sugary Christmas nonsense. Santa eats the pumpkin pie, the coffee with sugar, and the tangerine, and then gets hyper and flies up the chimney. He needs it. We don't.

Follow the Dr. Smith's Low-Stress Diet at Christmas. When you are at a party, eat some protein first, then chew some raw vegetables, hold a glass of white wine in your hand, and do not eat the gingerbread men, the sugar cookies, or the fruitcake. Remember, if it looks good, don't eat it. It is all just decoration.

9

Help Can
Make It Happen

Humans are supposed to be cheerful, free of infections and allergies, neither too fat nor too thin, able to sleep well at night and awaken refreshed. They should have a few friends and a mate. Freedom from pain should be a birthright. Ability to enjoy social encounters and to anticipate and to appreciate new, exciting experiences should be considered part of the norm.

If one is not getting the full measure of life's experiences because his or her body is malfunctioning, it is probably time to seek a relative, a friend, or a therapist and get redirected. We must stop assuming that average is normal. We must pay attention to seemingly insignificant deviations from the norm as early in life as possible. We can then take steps to correct them with appropriate lifestyle changes before the symptoms coalesce and become a major disease requiring drugs, surgery, or heavy psychotherapy.

The professional you seek should be sympathetic and willing to help you arrive at a reasonable goal, however long it takes. He or she should provide information—in a nice way—about the success rates of the different available treatments. A therapist should be able to work out a plan after a consultation with you, something you are both comfortable with. Realistic goals should be set up depending on genetic, physiological, and lifestyle factors. No plan should be forced on you. Not only must you *want* to follow the plan; you must *be able* to follow the plan.

Your doctor should not assume that your problem is due to some psychological deviation. Nor should it be implied that you have a moral weakness. If you are heavy, I don't need to tell you that you are discriminated against (and even persecuted) at great cost to your sense of well-being. Your self-image is on the ropes. A doctor should not make you feel demeaned or vulnerable in the examining room. Feelings of helplessness suppress the immune system. (That may be a reason why the overweight are more susceptible to certain cancers.) The more control you have in your life, the better able you are to control your weight and resist disease.

If you find that the doctor's office gives you feelings of depression, anger, inferiority, or confusion, then grab your clothes and get out before the bill goes up any higher. You do not have a deformity; you have a condition—a symptom—whose cause needs to be tracked down.

When you make an appointment with a doctor, it would be prudent to ask the receptionist or office nurse if the doctor treats weight problems. Does he/she *like* to treat the obese? Does he/she have a standard diet for everyone? Does he/she have a consulting dietician who is stuck with the four-basic-food-groups approach? Does he/she use vitamins? Does he/she send people to consultants?

Don't set foot inside the door unless you get a few answers and feel confident with the answers you get.

I know and refer patients to a chiropractor in Portland who was a computer programmer and a biochemist before he got his degree in chiropractic. He does a standard examination, a chiropractic evaluation, blood tests, a Heidelberg stomach acid test, blood tests for allergies, and anything else he feels appropriate depending on the patient's story. The patient then writes down what he or she eats during a typical week. All this goes into the office computer and out rolls a ten-page booklet. It details the subject's strengths and weaknesses and suggests therapy. This chiropractor tries to use only herbs, vitamins, and minerals. He balances the body. His thoughtfulness and concern are big factors in his rather high success rate. The so-called straight chiropractors only do adjustments of the spine and are uncomfortable suggesting supplements. The more liberal ones have found, however, that the patients get well more easily if a more holistic approach is used.

You may be able to get effective help from a naturopathic doctor, but they are not found in every state. They have special training in the physiology of digestion and the beneficial effects of the different herbs and natural remedies. They study anatomy, physiology, biochemistry, pathology, and are supervised in clinical instruction. Their studies last four years. My friend Dr. Wayne Anderson feels that cleansing the intestines and supporting the liver are key factors in balancing the body.

Psychotherapy may be an important treatment modality. It is expensive, but if everything else has been tried and your self-image is shot, this may be a turning point in your life.

You could dip into a new and not completely accepted (by orthodox medicine) science called kinesiology, also known as muscle-testing. The theory is that we all have an aura about us and that negative forces such as sickness, drugs, processed food, pollutants, and positive ions will distort this aura. Kirlian photography seems to demonstrate it. Call this aura what you will: perhaps the biochemicoelectromagnetic manifestation of our soul. (Well, there must be some internal force that keeps us alive.) The aura is tested by placing substances—foods, vitamins, minerals, drugs—near or on the body. Various muscles will respond to these forces by becoming weak or strong. I find it helpful; I have a friend who tests some of my patients, and together we can adjust their therapies more accurately. If your doctor groans when you ask him or her about it, better cross it off the list of things to do today.

The benefits of acupuncture and hypnosis are now legend. These modalities of treatment would best serve the patient who *really* finds it impossible to get off sugar or chocolate or ice cream or cigarettes. The benefits of these or any other technique will not last, however, unless the lifestyle is also changed. Exercise and the switch to nutrient-dense foods must accompany the above.

Many have reached their weight goals with the help of Weight Watchers, TOPS, and the other behavior modification groups. There is no doubt about their effectiveness, but the dropout rate is high, and these people may need the more personal attention of an empathetic health professional.

Although many doctors have made efforts to be more thoughtful, supportive, and sympathetic, the consumers/patients in our medical delivery system are beginning to realize that they can, or *must*, play a more vigorous role in the care of their own bodies. They are aware and appreciative of their own doctor's ability and conscientiousness, but they realize this medical mentor was not trained to encourage a preventive approach. The medical doctor (M.D.) was trained to diagnose the disease and prescribe the treatment. Take it or leave it. Do not embarrass the doctor by insisting on his or her recommending some preventive or alternative approach to your illness or condition if he or she doesn't respond positively to your questions. Most aren't aware of the alternatives themselves.

The point of this chapter is to make you realize that you do have choices. You want to lose the symptom of overweight. Be aware that there are people trained to help you—supportive professionals who will believe that inside all the fat is the real you trying desperately to get out.

By seeking the right help, you become your own number one health facilitator.

And that is how it should be!

Epilogue:
Health Should Be
a Birthright

A patient, a thirty-four-year-old woman, described her medical history, which began with a series of infections and allergies in adolescence. Then she developed asthma, and after being married for a few years and having a child she fell apart with colitis which seemed so devastating at the time that her colon was removed. When she came to me she was weak, wheezy, and depressed. The early stress had led to the diseases and the surgery, and these were so stressful that the diseases were perpetuated. The woman cannot get healthy until she is healthy. Vitamins and calcium shots have allowed her to sleep, get rid of her asthma, digest her food, and feel reasonably normal again.

But she is a mother, remember, and it is likely that her child, being the product of a stressful pregnancy, will herself be more susceptible to allergies and stress. Allergic children are more likely to be sickly, wakeful, touchy, and prone to ear and throat infections. The infections further deplete the body of

161

nutrients and thus the immune system is compromised. Allergies progress. Infections recur. A vicious circle.

Is it possible that this cycle could have been stopped twenty years ago, in this woman's adolescence? Might the last two decades of her life have been free of allergy, infection, pain, surgery, and general misery if someone had helped her immune system back then with a little preventive nutrition? Could she have suspected that her body was going to disintegrate? Or that her child would come into the world at risk for the same symptoms and diseases?

This book is about one particular symptom: obesity. When we have to admit to ourselves that we are overweight, then we must take heed of what the body is saying. Obesity is a sign that the body is experiencing stress.

The woman's story illustrates what can happen when we disregard the body's messages. It should help to explain why the weight management program described in this book is a total approach: if we eat appropriately, exercise moderately, follow a sane lifestyle, and alleviate the stresses in our lives, the symptom of obesity will almost certainly disappear. The solution to one symptom is the solution to all symptoms. We get healthy by getting healthy. By achieving this in our lives we give our children—who inherit our genes and our lifestyle—the best possible chance to enjoy health and long life and to pass that well-being on to the *next* generation.

Unfortunately, there is no snappy, universal answer that fits every plump person's problem. Obesity is multifactoral; the differences in outcome among the different treatment subgroups must be due to differences in the composition of the groups studied. Research by the experts is helping to define these subgroups and to establish guidelines for ideal weight depending on a particular person's physiology. But you alone live inside your body. No matter how much is learned about the causes and cures of obesity, it won't change the fact that you are your own number one health facilitator.

A couple of years ago my internist noted a change in my weight pattern. I had gone from my usual 170 pounds (1950 to 1980) to 180 pounds in 1981 and 190 pounds in 1982. He looked me in the eye and said, as kindly as he could, "What does this mean?" A provocative question.

I responded, "I am eating the same and exercising the same. What do you think?"

"You are getting older," he chuckled (he is a year older than I.) "And your metabolism is not as efficient as it used to be."

I cut back on wheat and cheese, my allergens. I lost 5 pounds in a week. I am taking 4 grains of thyroid because my temperature was 97.4°. I feel good because I feel good, but part of this is the knowledge that I have some personal control over my body. I know how and what to eat to control my energy level and my weight. I know what supplements to take and what foods to avoid. I am living in such a way to avoid the family curse of high blood pressure.

I don't mean to sound smug. I want you to see that you have options in maintaining your body: *you* can manage *it*, and make it and you feel good. Everyone should know about the physiology of the body so he or she will be able to maintain it in a state of well-being. We should be educating our population, from the earliest years of grade school, in the principles of health and nutrition. Learning to read and understand what the body is saying should be part of our cultural heritage.

Our children have to live inside their bodies all their lives. They may not need complete knowledge of the biochemical workings of the body, but they should know what diet and exercise can do. They should know how food sensitivities manifest themselves and what they can do to support their immune system. They should know the meaning of various physical and mental symptoms: that a colicky baby may be low in calcium, magnesium, or B_6; that a pimply adolescent with white spots on his or her nails is in need of zinc; that a depressed new mother needs vitamin B_{12}; that muscle cramps usually mean a calcium deficiency—despite an adequate milk intake. A fatigued person of any age should know that stress might be causing the fatigue, but that the B-complex vitamins might help.

This knowledge is not too difficult to acquire. It has allowed me to take charge of my life.

You can learn to do it, too.

Appendix:
The Page Clinic's
Super Seven
Food Plan

I have been so delighted with the results I get when I have people try the ideas from the Page Clinic, I want to reproduce them here for anyone who is determined to get some weight off and be comfortable, cheerful, and reasonably free of gas at the same time.

The Page Clinic in Saint Petersburg Beach, Florida, has found that the following way of life seems to help all comers. As you will see, it keeps sugar, fat, and dairy products to a minimum and teaches people how to sequence their food. They do other things than just marching through the garden nibbling. They provide psychological supports, they get people to exercise, they diagnose endocrine imbalances and treat those; in short, they provide a holistic approach to diseases. They feel there is no special diet for each of the nasties: cancer, or overweight or allergies or arthritis or depression or coronary artery disease. They feel that if the body is balanced and the homeostasis is supported, then most of the symptoms and signs of illness will disappear.

This approach is called the Page Super Seven Food Plan. You are to prepare and eat only tablespoon-size portions. Choose only one food from each category. Vegetarians who combine beans and grains may have a double portion of those foods. Steam the vegetables. Kelp powder, sea salt, plain pepper, and raw butter are allowed to season the foods. You may eat as many meals a day as you like. Meals may be called snacks, if you like. But do space them at least two or more hours apart. The protein is eaten first to take advantage of the stomach acid. The digestive efficiency of the intestines is at its optimum if the seven groups of foods are eaten in the following sequence:

Category 1: Complete Protein. Egg, chicken, duck, turkey, beef, lamb, mollusk, crustaceans, pork, combinations of beans and grains.

Category 2: Legume and Grain Combinations. Beans: adzuki, black-eyed, kidney, lima, pinto, navy, soy, green peas, chick peas, lentils, snap peas, snow peas, string beans. Grains: barley, brown rice, buckwheat, oats, millet, wheat berries, rye.

Category 3: Root Vegetables. Beet, carrot, Jerusalem artichoke, kohlrabi, onion, parsnip, potato, rutabaga, turnip.

Category 4: Yellow or White Vegetables. Cauliflower, fresh corn, cucumber, onion, parsnip, radish, rutabaga, acorn squash, hubbard squash, turnip.

Category 5: Green Vegetables. Artichoke, asparagus, broccoli, celery, endive, green pepper, leek, okra, scallion, snap peas, snow peas, sprouts, string beans, zucchini.

Category 6: Red, Orange, and Purple Vegetables. Beet, carrot, eggplant, pumpkin, red pepper, butternut squash, sweet potato, tomato, purple cabbage.

Category 7: Green Leafy Vegetables. Bok choy, cabbage, kale, lettuce, mustard greens, parsley, spinach, Swiss chard, turnip greens, watercress, sprouts (mung and alfalfa), beet tops, Brussels sprouts, endive.

Dr. Lorenzani points out the chief problem when attempting to follow this sequencing of foods, prudent though it may be. "Obviously this could lead to hysteria if one is eating soup or shredded salads. In this case, just follow the basic rule of eating the protein first, if possible. In restaurants, salads are usually served far in advance of the protein. Can you sit for 15 minutes and stare at the fluffy colorful concoction without your fork meandering in the direction of the bowl? Maybe not. Why not ask that your salad be served with the main course? Then save it for dessert!"

The patients at the Page Clinic learn the art of planning in advance so that eating, relaxation, drinking water, and exercise are all included in the day's activity. Now that's holistic. Overweight patients have found that weight loss is effortless, but they have also learned a new lifestyle. Health skills are now a habit pattern. See if you can follow their method for a week. You must remember, tablespoon-size portions. Low-calorie dressings are made with oil, water, lemon juice, garlic, and herbs.

Here would be a few days of the Page Clinic Diet:

DAY 1

Breakfast	Lunch	Dinner
soft boiled egg	tuna	beef and vegetable
millet	kidney beans	soup
kidney beans	tomato	ground sirloin
onion	onion	kidney beans
sweet potato	cucumber	carrot
carrot	radishes	tomato
Brussels sprouts	leaf lettuce	onion
spinach		green pepper

Snacks: carrot sticks, radishes, cucumber slices

DAY 2

Breakfast	Lunch	Dinner
Boston scrod	(Stir in wok with a	(Vegetarian meal)
barley	little butter):	brown rice
lentils	chicken breast	lentils
yellow squash	brown rice	beets
parsnips	lentil sprouts	butternut squash
purple cabbage	parsnips	celery
string beans	celery	turnip root
parsley	yellow squash	
	eggplant cubes	

Snacks: celery sticks, yellow squash, turnip roots

Day 3

Breakfast	Lunch	Dinner
turkey breast	(Cook in wok):	lamb
brown rice	shrimp	oats
lentil sprouts	brown rice	potato
parsnips	lentil sprouts	green peas
purple cabbage	green beans	(Salad of):
corn	yellow squash	alfalfa sprouts
zucchini	parsnips	radishes
parsley	eggplant cubes	red pepper
	endive salad	green cabbage

The above diet would allow the serious-minded dieter to find his or her comfortable diet; one that he or she can stick with and not get bored. Germans would get the cabbage and potatoes and pork in there. Orientals might find this diet is much to their taste, and the main thing they would learn is to use *brown rice* for heaven's sake, and eat the protein first. We are all truly different, and one man's nectar may be another's poison. But I hope you have learned some basic rules to follow.

Index

171

About the Author

Dr. Lendon Smith has been practicing pediatrics since 1951. During the past nine years he has particularly emphasized nutritional counseling for parents. Dr. Smith is former Clinical Professor of Pediatrics at the University of Oregon Medical School and a member of the American Academy of Pediatrics. He first became a favorite of television viewers for his show *The Children's Doctor*—also the title of his first book—and won an Emmy for his television documentary *My Mom's Having a Baby*. Dr. Smith is a frequent guest on the major network television shows and is the author of the best-selling *Improving Your Child's Behavior Chemistry*, *Feed Your Kids Right*, *Foods for Healthy Kids*, and *Feed Yourself Right*. Dr. Smith is currently seen once a week on Hearst/ABC Video Services' Daytime programming. Dr. Smith and his wife live in Portland, Oregon.